Happy Birthday Lovely

You Truly Are Amazing x

Make Money Online

Dearest Lou +

April 2023! When The Dream Began!

Looking forward to seeing you + your company flourish! You Are Amazing!

Huge hug + lots of love!

Jackie xxx

For Finnian and Albert

LISA JOHNSON

Make Money Online

YOUR NO-NONSENSE GUIDE TO PASSIVE INCOME

First published in Great Britain in 2023 by Yellow Kite
An imprint of Hodder & Stoughton
An Hachette UK company

3

Copyright © Lisa Johnson 2023

A CIP catalogue record for this title is
available from the British Library

Trade Paperback ISBN 978 1 399 70192 1
eBook ISBN 978 1 399 70193 8

Typeset in Freight Text by Hewer Text UK Ltd, Edinburgh
Printed and bound in Great Britain by Clays Ltd, Elcograf S.p.A.

Hodder & Stoughton policy is to use papers that are
natural, renewable and recyclable products and made
from wood grown in sustainable forests. The logging and
manufacturing processes are expected to conform to the
environmental regulations of the country of origin.

Yellow Kite
Hodder & Stoughton Ltd
Carmelite House
50 Victoria Embankment
London EC4Y 0DZ

www.yellowkitebooks.co.uk

You can't. I can.
You'll fail. I might.
You'll quit. I won't.

CONTENTS

Foreword by Andrea McLean

Three little words . . . Make. Money. Online.

Three little words that instantly polarise, because of what they represent to the reader. Anger, disgust, jealousy?

Or – curiosity, optimism, hope?

It's simply not British to talk so openly about a desire to make money. Or worse, to discuss making money online. It smacks of the Wild West and it's unsettling because it's misunderstood and therefore not to be trusted.

I get it. That's how I felt when I left the career I had known and understood, having worked in it for a quarter of a century, to venture into the online space. I did it because I wanted to make a difference and I wanted to use my passion and skillset to help others – and online was the best way to do this. In fact, it was the only way to do it at the time, as we were in the middle of a global pandemic and in-person meetings or events were not possible.

Our need to make money is a basic one. Unless you are blessed to possess that magical tree on which currency grows, you will have to find a way to pay to keep a roof over your head, and to feed and clothe yourself. That much is understood. As is the notion that success comes from the amount of time you personally spend working. But we are fortunate to be living in a time when the online world offers the opportunity to step away from this linear concept, giving us the opportunity to offer our unique skillset not just to our employer, or our direct customers, but to the world.

This is what Lisa outlines so clearly in this book, as she explains through her own experience and the many examples of those she has personally coached: your skills are worth something, because of what you bring to them. Yes, other people may have them, too, but they don't have your take on them. And your take on things may be exactly what someone needs right now. In the same way that we choose our favourite hairdresser or restaurant because there is something about how they do things that we like, regardless of the fact that there are countless others we could have chosen.

So how do you take a skill that works in the real world and transfer it to the online space? And can anyone do it? Within reason, yes – although obviously not in a like-for-like way. The key thing to remember is: just because something seems obvious and easy to you doesn't mean it is obvious or easy to someone else. You can help them to understand it by teaching them about it. And then it is something you can turn into a business.

Will it work for everyone? Pretty much, yes.

Will it make you rich? Perhaps, depending on what you are offering, how good you are at it and how much time you're willing to commit to doing it – at least initially.

What Lisa brings you in this book is a step-by-step guide to taking something you already do offline, showing you how you can make money from it online. There are no gimmicks, no trickery, no one-size-fits-all cookie-cutter get-rich-quick schemes. With straight-talking warmth, she simply shows you how you too can Make Money Online.

Andrea McLean
CEO and Co-Founder of This Girl is On Fire

Introduction

You're now holding my book. A book that I actually wrote! Of course, this is hardly an earth-shattering revelation, but the fact that we have arrived at this scenario still blows my mind.

The trajectory of my journey could be described as 'unconventional', and yet here we are, just you and me and thousands of words for you to digest.

My life began forty-four years ago in a council house in a small Lincolnshire town. The middle one of three, I was, without doubt, a complicated, slightly awkward child. Yet despite this awkwardness, I was a pretty bright kid (some might go so far as to call me clever!). I possessed a very clear understanding of what was right and what was wrong and was prepared to discuss these beliefs with anyone who thought otherwise (nothing has changed in this respect). Along with this came a healthy dose of stubbornness, meaning that if something was started, it would be finished (again, no change there).

However, my childhood and a large percentage of my adult life were challenging for a number of reasons that will become clearer as you read on. I'm hoping that you *will* read on, as there are plenty of tales to be told and heaps of business gold.

After finishing school with a handful of mediocre GCSEs and leaving the Mormon religion I'd grown up in, I was married and living on a chicken farm at eighteen. My self-esteem had been shattered (I'll go into that later), so I'd looked for the quickest route to love and normalcy, and marriage to the first person who showed an interest was my own (rather poor) choice. Divorce number one happened at age twenty-one.

Let's now skip through a variety of careers, qualifications and adventures, including chicken farming, waitressing, personal assistant, tutoring, banking and more, until, in 2011, I was joined in the world by two tiny bundles of noise, mess and pure joy. Enter Albert and Finnian, my not-completely-planned little life-changers.

With the benefit of hindsight, this momentous event can now perhaps be looked on as my Ground Zero moment. I had scrappily worked my way up to a career as a risk analyst in the City, starting out as the office junior and proving myself over a number of years, doing rather well, considering where I'd started, and working crazy hours. I went back to this job when the twins were five months old and it became clear that it just wasn't going to logistically work. The juggle of not sleeping and working in a job where I was supposed to be 'on it' from 7am to 9pm was killing me, and I never saw the twins!

Instead, I found a job five minutes' walk from my house working as a PA for a female CEO – quite stress-free, but also frustratingly challenge-free. I went about my business efficiently and professionally, but fulfilled is not how I would describe myself back then. So what to do? I knew I couldn't go back to the City life, but I also knew that in the words of Ralph Waldo Emerson: 'The mind, once stretched by a new idea, never returns to its original dimensions'. And my mind felt pretty stretched.

I decided quite quickly (this will become a recurring theme, you'll see) to start a business. But what business did I want to run? I liked parties, celebrations and nights out, so the obvious choice was to become a wedding and events planner. By all accounts, cake was involved, so of course it was ideal!

Carmela Weddings was launched while I was going through divorce number two (Carmela is my middle name and a little nod to my Maltese roots), with a basic website and no discernible knowledge of how to actually plan a wedding. But aided by a healthy dose of tenacity and a mind that learned quickly, the business snowballed and soon we were fully booked for the next year, which was a good thing because the divorce, the less lucrative job and the two more mouths to feed had left me in £30k worth of credit-card debt.

At the end of the first year, I sat down and did the sums. After all that work, I had only earned £1.15 an hour. I didn't understand what I was doing wrong, and I was never going to be able to pay off my debt. At this point I was working with any client I could lay my hands on, which meant village halls, doilies on tables, sweetie carts, chair covers . . . But that wasn't what I wanted. I wanted the cool couples, the warehouse weddings, the modern design. And I wanted to start earning decent money.

Discovering Business Coaches

It was then that I found out that business coaches were a 'thing' and I had to make a choice: hire one and get into more debt (£5k to be precise) or give up on the crazy dreams to do more with my life and realise I would have to live hand to mouth and in debt, as so many generations of my family had done before me. I bit the bullet and hired the coach, but with a promise to myself that it was non-negotiable to make that money back.

I listened and I learned and I implemented, and, with a rebrand and a fresh approach, within months I was still fully booked – *but this time with clients who were perfect for me and who were paying me significantly more.*

My success did not go unnoticed and my fellow wedding professionals started approaching me to ask how I had done it. How had I grown so quickly in such a short space of time to be fully booked with ideal clients? Then other small business owners contacted me, too. Being a generous person, I helped them all out. I told them what I'd done and how I'd done it. By this point, I was a business learning junkie. I'd read all the books and gone to every free webinar and I told all these people everything I'd learned. They too started to see increases in bookings, and I made a bit of a name for myself as the 'go-to' business success story who explained things in an easy-to-understand way.

Incredibly, I started to slowly pay off my debt. And it also needs to be pointed out that I did all of this while juggling caring for toddler twins and a nine-to-five full-time job. I'm not going to pretend that this period of my life was easy, but I'll tell you how I managed later in the book.

Lightbulb Moments

About a year after starting the business, I had two moments that could perhaps be described as epiphanies, or, at the very least, lightbulb moments.

1 I started my wedding business to increase my income and to create more freedom in my life while doing something I enjoyed. However, I hadn't really thought this through: wedding season starts in the spring and runs right through to the end of summer, which is the time I like to travel and spend time with my twins. The average wedding takes 200 hours to plan properly, and then the event itself usually runs from the Friday through to the Sunday. These events take place every weekend from April to September. In hindsight, it wasn't a well-thought-out business model for me.

2 I was providing strategic advice to other business owners, which they were all using to improve their businesses. I was actually helping them to make more money. Surely if *they* used this advice to become more successful, there would be others who would also benefit from my help. And, well, maybe pay me for it.

The upshot of these two bursts of inspiration was that there had to be a link. A way to utilise the skills I'd acquired and was now passing on to others while, at the same time, not spending every weekend and evening working, so I could actually have some quality time with my family while the sun was (occasionally) shining.

My Consulting Business Launch

In 2017, I launched my consulting business, expanding the depth and detail of the advice and strategy I was offering to fledgling online businesses. I was successful straight away; and, if you don't mind, I'll take a moment for a humble brag here about how I earned £220k in revenue that first year because of all the business knowledge I'd acquired. (Don't worry, I'm going to reveal it all to you in this book!)

The success was exhilarating and financially rewarding, but hugely exhausting, and I'd slipped right back into the habit of not spending much time with my kids. Ultimately, I had left that nine-to-five job for a 6am–11pm business. Also, I could never earn any more money because I was fully booked every day with clients and working to full capacity.

I loved what I was doing, what I was teaching and who I was working with. Most of all, I loved seeing my clients learning, thriving and making a success of their businesses – the rewards were immeasurable.

But this was not going to plan. How, then, could I increase my reach and supercharge my earnings, while simultaneously decreasing my hours and having more of a social life (and find the time to go on some dates with the new man I was seeing)?

Discovering the Power of Passive Income

One day I was listening to a heated debate on a podcast about something called 'passive income'. I regarded it warily, with preconceptions of pyramid schemes and shady

MLM set-ups (this stands for multi-level marketing and I'll talk about it in Chapter 1) that did not sit comfortably with me, but I investigated it nonetheless. And I went down a rabbit hole!

I discovered that this slightly misleading and often misinterpreted heading of 'passive income' covered a great deal more than meets the eye. Passive income means different things to different people, and it is not a new concept but, in essence, it's about avoiding reaching a point where you can't take on more customers because you've run out of hours in the day.

I felt like this could be the way forward, giving me more freedom. I decided to spend half of the profit I had made and invest it in signing up to the best coaches and courses specialising in passive income.

Over the course of 2018, I started introducing some passive income streams. By the end of year two, everything had changed. I had gone from working eighty hours a week to only seven and a half and was bringing in over £1m in revenue.

I remembered a great quote I'd read somewhere by industrial engineer Allen F. Morgenstern, along the lines of 'Work smarter, not harder' – and that became my ethos.

That business is now in its fourth year and, so far, it has made over £7m. And I still work just thirty hours a month. I travel for most of the year, with my husband, who works for me, and my twins. I have grown the little business that started on my coffee table five years ago to a team of nine lovely people. I have also made lots of mistakes along the way – that is just an inevitable part of owning a business – but I'll tell you all about them, too, so you don't make the same errors.

What Can You Expect From This Book?

In Chapters 1 and 2, I'm going to tell you what passive income is and talk you through a really easy system I devised to help you understand what is needed, with examples of various types of income streams to explain the difference between passive and semi-passive income. We'll then go deep into money mindset in Chapter 3; I can't wait for you to read this one because it can change everything for you when you know how you might be stopping yourself attracting in money. In Chapter 4, we'll focus on the easiest type of passive income to get started – courses and memberships – which leads nicely into growing an audience in Chapter 5 (an important task, regardless of which income stream you choose). In Chapters 6 and 7, we'll delve into how to find your ideal clients and the systems online that are going to make your life easier (it's the techy bit, but I promise I've kept it simple!). Then, Chapter 8 – my favourite part – is all about launching your offering to the world. We end with Chapter 9 and some real talk on ethics and integrity, so that you can sleep easy at night.

And now here we are, back to you holding my book in your hands. A book I've been given the privilege to write. A book in which yes, I will talk about how passive income works, but also so much more than that.

I'll teach you how to grow your business, to grow your audience, to pinpoint that ideal client and keep them engaged. I'll share loads of helpful information and simple, step-by-step plans to help you get to where you want to be with your business life without sacrificing your personal one. And all while being honest, open and ethical.

So a massive thank you to you for reading this, and let's get cracking with helping you make more money while doing less stuff.

CHAPTER 1

Introducing Passive Income and the CASsH® System

Whenever I read books by inspirational business leaders, they always seem to include anecdotes about how when they were kids, they came up with really ingenious ideas to make money, giving a clear indication that their entrepreneurial spirit was an innate gift and it was never in doubt that they would go on to achieve greatness.

I always reacted with a 'Meh, whatever' kind of response to these tales, thinking they had been embellished to create a kind of 'benefit-of-hindsight' explanation for their success. But recently, as I was thinking about penning this book, I began to realise that I too have some similarly themed anecdotes in my locker! They generally involve me as a bored yet aspirational teen, coming up with some sure-fire business success idea and roping my sister, Marie, and best friend, Hazel, in to do the legwork, while I sat and 'supervised'. This included cleaning cars, a paper round and a short-lived venture as Avon ladies aged fourteen. (As an aside, these two characters are now working for me and may well feature again in the course of this book.)

But there is one venture that I had forgotten about until I sat down to write this book, and it was perhaps my most successful. I had, and still have, a pretty near photographic memory. I am fortunate in that if I see something written down, it is then committed to memory, which suited the English schooling system pretty well, as it is mostly (and erroneously, in my eyes) based on the ability to remember facts and then write them down in an exam scenario.

At the age of twelve, I had the brainwave of creating a small 'crib sheet' for exam questions, with some nice, neat little bullet points and tips that could easily be absorbed and recalled by most students and used to expand their answers when they took the exam. Of course, I couldn't guarantee that their exam questions would be the same as the ones I'd used, but there was a good chance that the points I mentioned would still be useful.

I got Hazel to print the sheets off on the photocopier at her dad's office, and I then sold them to my fellow students for 20p or thereabouts. This proved quite profitable – until word got around and they realised they could just share one sheet!

But on reflection, this was my first foray into what I would come to know as 'passive income': one product, created once by me, and sold to a number of different end users.

Four simple words: trading time for money.

Think about the meaning of these four simple words. You are trading your most valuable asset – the one thing that you know for sure you can never get any more of – for cash. Let's analyse what this means in its simplest sense.

For the purposes of this section, I want you to choose someone you know, someone who runs their own business, is an entrepreneur or a sole trader, rather than someone who is employed by an organisation.

I'll use my friend Michael who is a personal trainer as an example. (I should have said he is *my* personal trainer to sound all healthy and posh, but this would be a lie. I am neither of those things.)

Michael is doing well. He has lots of clients and he carries out personal-training sessions every day. But what he doesn't have enough of is time. He has other potential clients who would like to work with him, but he just cannot fit them in. He literally doesn't have enough hours in the day. In basic terms, he is turning down money that people would like to pay him.

Now, I don't know about you, but to me that seems like a fundamental error. But what can be done to resolve this conundrum? We have no flux capacitor or means to expand the day from twenty-four to thirty-six or forty-eight hours.

So what then? In essence, it's a very simple solution:

Instead of one to one, think one to many.

In other words, rather than only ever serving one client at a time, we can create a model that provides the same or a similar service to many people at the same time. No more one to one, but instead one to many.

Other than my short-lived exam-sheet adventure, the first time that I was aware of coming across something that could definitely be labelled as passive income was when I was trying to organise a holiday to Disneyland for a friend who was juggling little kids and a job. I said I'd help out.

Now, I don't know if you have tried to do this, but it is more like a military operation than most military operations. Even once you've decided on a hotel, there are endless choices for breakfasts, lunches, fast-track passes and packages to ensure that you and your little ones don't miss out on anything.

I'd honestly thought she could rock up at the park, wander in, get on some rides and grab Mickey for an autograph. But a quick Google search revealed that this could not be further from the truth. There were numerous chat rooms full of advice, most talking of planning for months before your trip and creating an elaborate spreadsheet to guide you through your 'relaxing' holiday.

In one of these rooms, I came across a lady who was selling a PDF called something like 'Making Disney easy with kids under 4' for £49. This was precisely what I needed, so I snapped it up and got cracking with planning the trip, still feeling slightly daunted, but at least knowing how it all worked. All the information was now in one easy-to-reference place, which, crucially, meant no more trawling the Internet.

When I wrote to the lady who had created the sheet to say thanks, we ended up chatting about how it came to be a thing. She had been in my shoes and could find nothing that answered all her questions. After her visit, she simply wrote down everything she had learned, and drafted it up into the PDF that was now in my possession.

She wrote it once. She sold a few every month, more at busy times, and made regular recurring revenue through-out the year without having to do anything. It wasn't millions, but to quote her, 'It's a nice contribution towards the cost of our next trip'.

A seed had been sown.

What Passive Income Really Means

The simple explanation of passive income is this: *not trading time for money*. It is not a new concept. People have been making passive income for years but not calling it that. I think the Internet and social media have made the term more widely known, but it's always been there.

Think of it as building or making something (we'll call this the asset – look at us, using proper investment terms!) and then making money from it, over and over again, without needing to put in more work or more time.

Let's look at the most basic situation.

If you rent a room in your house, this is passive income. Think about it. You already have the room (your asset) and then you make the asset more valuable by putting a bed in it and decorating it nicely with maybe a wardrobe or chest of drawers. You then put an ad in your local paper that you have a room to rent (marketing your asset). You have now done the hard work. Then someone lives in the room and pays you a few hundred pounds every month. You are doing nothing else, yet you are making money every month from your asset. You are making passive income because you are no longer trading time for money; instead, you're trading the asset for money.

Dispelling the Myths Around Passive Income

If I had a pound for every time I've heard someone say 'passive income doesn't exist', I'd be writing this book from my Hollywood Hills mansion.

I think the underlying reason for this is that the catch-all heading of 'passive income' is slightly misleading. (Yes, I know I use it a lot, but it still frustrates me because there isn't a better one. I've tried 'leveraged income', but it still doesn't quite tick the boxes and nobody knows what I'm talking about.) And there are many online articles and podcast episodes 'debunking' it.

Comments such as these are common:

The passive income myth has taken the Internet by storm. As a seasoned investment manager, I'm repeatedly astonished by the percentage of people that believe the passive income myth.

I could never understand how well-educated people are spreading this myth as a religion or, even better, cult. Of course, I have in mind people with good intentions, not the ones selling some education programme or investment product.
Business passive income is a lie.

It's one of those myths that has been perpetuated for so long by so many experts we no longer question its validity . . . even though we should. After all, who wouldn't want an endless stream of cash flowing into their bank account without lifting a finger? That's the passive income promise, and it has wide appeal.

We'll come back to this shortly. But let's take a look at some other reasons for the widespread scepticism around passive income.

PYRAMID SCHEMES AND MLMS

Most of us will have heard of, come across or even worked within the world of pyramid schemes or MLMs.

A pyramid scheme is a fraudulent system of making money based on recruiting an ever-increasing number of 'investors'. It is so called because the number of investors increases at each level.

Pyramid schemes are businesses that recruit people whose job it is to enrol others into the scheme, rather than selling an actual product or service. The nature of the business model means that a few people at the 'top' of the pyramid end up earning money, while the large number at the 'bottom' make little to none.

Pyramid schemes are illegal in the UK.

While similar in structure to a pyramid scheme, an MLM is not illegal and there is a product involved. The product can be anything, often skincare or beauty goods.

BRO MARKETING

Then there is the shadow that hangs over the sales methods used to promote a number of passive income products. The unethical and, well, just nasty tactics employed by what have become known as 'bro marketers'.

On her podcast, Melbourne-based marketing coach Rachel Kurzyp describes bro marketing as 'gross and sleazy car salesman tactics that we all know and hate. In a nutshell, bro marketing is self-serving, short-term-gain sales tactics that are used to disempower clients and remove a customer's agency so that they can be easily manipulated into buying a service or product.'*

Bro marketers tend to use one-time offers and bait, such as 'only twenty minutes to buy', to trigger consumers' desire. This means that the logic that should be applied to a buying decision (is it affordable? Is it really needed?) is often overridden by the fear of missing out on a one-time opportunity.

Unethical but often successful, these tactics are the very antithesis of what I stand for, yet they remain at the forefront of how people view the passive income world and what it looks like.

We often hear those pesky bro marketers spouting lines such as 'make money while you just sleep'. (**Note:** don't think all bro marketers are men. The title refers to the technique, not the gender, and the technique is regularly used by women in equally unscrupulous ways.) Excuse me while I pause for a few seconds to roll my eyes, shake my head and tut loudly.

Ok, moving on.

Non-believers like to make out that we're suggesting you don't have to lift a finger to make this money, but that's not true – and it's definitely not what most passive income advocates, myself included, would say. (And I don't think a single person in the world would believe someone who said

* https://rachelkurzyp.com.au/2021/02/17/bro-marketing-explained/

that anyway.) Theirs is a dangerous message because, truth alert: any form of passive or semi-passive income (and I'll go into these concepts in more detail in Chapter 2) requires plenty of work at the beginning. Of course it does. There is no 'secret', no magic wand to wave at the clouds so that cash rains down on you.

You will need a level of promotion, advertising and audience building, depending on how successful you want to be – all the things that pretty much any business needs to become financially successful. But, and I stand by this 100 per cent, by following some pretty clear steps and putting some effort in, *absolutely anyone can make passive and semi-passive income.* And it's worth that effort.

Yet so many people are put off starting their own business because they feel they don't have any kind of specialist knowledge. Even if they have a skill, they are sure that no one will pay them money to find out what is already in their heads.

This is the stumbling block for many of my clients when I first work with them. But once we delve deeper into their backstories, their experiences, their interests, there is always something. Something that they know about. Something that excites them. They just need to remember one of the most important adages for anyone creating a one-to-many model of business:

Your knowledge is not common knowledge.

Often, we have an area of expertise – be it knitting, dogs, knitting dogs (I bet that's a thing!), cooking, parenting – or any of the countless sectors that provide income streams to thousands of businesses. But we forget that not everyone knows what we know. That's precisely why we have to dig deep into those knowledge pockets and use what we find there to shape what we are going to create.

My definition of an expert is simply this: the person who knows the most about a particular subject in an average-sized room. Not a football stadium, not a cinema, not even a large room.

Let that sink in and now we'll move on to the other main reasons 'not to do it'.

What's Stopping You?

Well, I'm no psychic, but it usually stems from a couple of main reasons.

REASON NUMBER 1

The all-consuming belief that we as individuals struggle to overcome is that we will never be the 'go-to guru', the 'number-one knowledge base' in our area of expertise. Seriously, not everyone can be Tony Robbins or Oprah. They are just the ones with the headlines and the plaudits. But I'll bet that in your group of friends you are the 'go-to guru' for something – anything from knowing the best cocktail bars to being a human satnav. (**Note:** I am firmly in the camp of the first of these examples.) I also bet that you have no problem assuming this role with enthusiasm.

Which leads us neatly on to . . .

. . . REASON NUMBER 2

The classic 'But it's all been done before'. Well, of course it has. If it hasn't been done by somebody, sometime before, that's a pretty clear indication that it may well not be a very good idea and you should have a serious rethink!

I like to apply what I call the 'Brick Lane Analogy' here, named after the street in East London that is approximately 1 mile long and home to around twenty-five Indian restaurants. In theory, this does not appear to be a recipe for success, yet all these establishments thrive in close proximity to each other. And this is because they each have their individual appeal, their own take on Indian food, their specific target audience. Their unique selling point (USP). Yes, they offer the same product, but each puts their own spin on it. Much like the pubs, hairdressers and nail bars dotted throughout almost every high street in the country.

This analogy is even more applicable to a passive- or semi-passive income business. Because online, as you start to build your audience, it is *your* personality that will be your main sales point.

People buy from people.

Actually, I'd go a step further. *People buy from people they like.*

I have an engaged and committed audience, and you will come to see that this is far more important than 'likes' or followers on social media. If I have made money from passive income, you can, too. *You* are most definitely enough.

How Passive Income Can Help *Anybody* Change Their Life

There are so many ways to create passive and semi-passive income streams in an ethical, efficient and profitable manner. I will talk about all of these in more depth in the next chapter, but the best way to start is to tap into your existing knowledge, so I will focus on that model for the next few sections.

I used to think the only people who could set up their own businesses and create a steady stream of recurring revenue were:

a) Old-school entrepreneurs; you know the type – they start off selling sweets to their school friends aged seven, buy their first house aged seventeen and they're millionaires aged twenty-three, working all the hours (they invented the paperclip or something).

b) Financial whizz kids with razor-sharp business acumen – trader types (they invested cryptocurrency, maybe).

c) Technological boffins who created some kind of hitherto-unheard-of-but-once-launched-cannot-be-lived-without service that changes the world (software or maybe Uber).

Now, I definitely don't fit into any of these categories. My youthful forays into business ventures as a kid were, much like my exam crib sheet (see p. 12), short-lived and unsustainable, resulting in an exhausted and demotivated workforce (my sister and friend).

I also know for a fact that there is no demographic for those who are successfully making passive or semi-passive income. My clients range from teenagers to seventy-five-year-olds, with hugely varying backgrounds. Some dropped out of school at fifteen, while some have masters' degrees. I have clients in over thirty countries and have worked with lawyers, dog trainers, cake makers, coaches, artists, hula hoopers and pretty much everything in between. The only trait that they all share – the factor that ties all these inspirational people together – is that they all experienced . . . the *'epiphany moment'*.

The epiphany moment was when each of them realised they possessed a skill or some knowledge that others would be interested in learning about. And this was when they recognised that they could make money from it, too.

DANI'S STORY

Dani Wallace is a real person, a client and friend of mine. She is a whirlwind of infectious energy and all-round inspirational human being for a bagful of reasons. She has overcome adversity in numerous forms to become one of the most sought-after motivational speakers in the United Kingdom.

But just a couple of years ago, Dani could barely afford to fill her car with petrol.

Dani was a singer and had also started doing speaking gigs on confidence. I was in Chicago when I received a message from her on Facebook; we'd never spoken before, but her message said, 'I need your help with something. You and me – we're going to be friends.' Let's just say I was curious enough to give her a call.

We chatted and she invited me to a charitable event that she had planned, but unfortunately, I was unable to attend. Something about her really resonated with me, though, so I invited her to join my online membership (I'd started this to bring together new business owners so they could learn about business in an affordable way), where she was massively engaged and super enthusiastic.

Not long after this, I was taking a short break in Malta and put it out on social media to see if any ladies fancied joining me there. (A bit of sun and a few daiquiris always work wonders!) Little did I know that Dani had seen this post and was already putting wheels in motion to ensure she would be there.

She found some cheap flights, and somehow managed to make it happen, despite having only £200 left to her name.

So we spent a few days, twelve of us, just relaxing, chatting, sharing, teaching, learning and supporting each other. Dani looked like she was having a great time; her effervescent personality and all-round enthusiasm meant she was a genuine pleasure to be around.

The day before we were due to fly back, we all spoke about what we were planning to do next in our businesses – what we were launching and any new ideas bubbling away.

I had mentioned my new programme – or mastermind – earlier, and when it came to Dani's turn to speak, she looked genuinely emotional and said something like, 'I don't know how, but I'm going to find the money to be part of that mastermind programme. I want to stop feeling so out of my depth, but I just don't know how to get to where you are.'

Now, I had witnessed the power of Dani for a few days, and I *knew* that she was destined for huge things. She just hadn't yet worked out how to get there.

'Ok,' I said. 'Let's have a look at this in a bit more detail and I'm going to work out how we are going to get you to where you deserve to be.'

We were at lunch, and I'd had half a bottle of wine by this point, but I grabbed a napkin and a pen and started scribbling down goals and figures and how much Dani wanted to earn. It soon became clear that, as discussed earlier, time was the issue here. She was a great singer and speaker, but she was limited by time. Only so many hours; only so many gigs.

But.

I pointed out to her that *teaching people to speak* was a whole different ball game. So many people have a real fear of public speaking. It is a massive block that really limits their potential to grow as business owners and as individuals.

So we focused on this. I helped her draft a rough outline of how to launch an online programme teaching people how to create and present awesome speeches. Then I asked her to remind me how much she wanted to make from it.

'£7k,' she said.

I had no doubt that this programme had the potential to make way more than this, and told her so, yet she still found it hard to believe that 'people like her' could make this kind of money by teaching something they love.

A few weeks later, her launch made £16k. From the back of a napkin to £16k. This was a life-changing sum for her at the time, and she did it without working all hours, driving around the country to speaking gigs. Plus, she was able to spend time with her kids.

A process and a plan were what made this a possibility.

But it was Dani's belief that made it a reality.

Then Covid hit and Dani was so grateful she had learned to make semi-passive income. With all gigs cancelled, Dani went on to make over £300k online and moved into her dream house during the pandemic.

Find out more about Dani at iamthequeenbee.co.uk

Why Social Media Has Made Passive Income More Popular and Easier Than Ever

We've all heard it said. You need to work all the hours there are to make money. Our parents drummed this into us. My dad definitely did. And from his experience as a single father with jobs that went on all night, I really believed it, too. Work all the hours to make the money, then, because you are working all the hours, there is no time left to enjoy the rewards that the money you have earned should bring. Until you retire, when you are too exhausted to enjoy it, anyway!

We have to understand that this thinking was far more applicable and truthful a generation or two ago. If you had a product, you needed to get it out there. Of course, this is still true, and I can't emphasise enough the importance of building an engaged and loyal audience, but we now have a world that has shrunk to the size of our phones or our laptops.

I was fortunate enough to enjoy a fabulous trip to Iceland a few years ago – a perk of working in the wedding industry. (I say a perk, but it was -18°C and I am not a cold-weather girl, but the Northern Lights made it worth the eight layers of clothing.) While there, we (there were eight businesses there in total) met up with some of the suppliers who could possibly be of use to us.

One character who has stayed with me ever since was a calm, friendly, unassuming guy called Gunnar who was a graphic designer. His family had always been artistic and had, in one way or another, worked in a creative industry. However, when he was a kid, his family packed up and moved from their remote corner of Iceland to Reykjavik, so they could engage with their audience throughout the year, ensuring a regular market for their artistic creations and design services.

Later, as Gunnar's business grew, he needed to meet with his clients, work out what their remit was and how he could create an end product that ticked all their boxes. He was happy, he enjoyed his work, but he never stopped missing the isolated, beautiful home of his youth, while feeling tied to the city by the income that it generated. Then, a few years ago, he realised two things.

Firstly, most of his communication with clients was now carried out over the Internet, and his audience was growing around the world, no longer restricted to Iceland. Secondly, he noticed he was being asked the same questions by many of his potential clients. A lot of them liked the idea of his services but couldn't afford to commit to a one-to-one bespoke service. So he set up a course. A beginner's guide to using graphic-design software and creating your own designs.

Gunnar created a low-cost offer that would help numerous clients, not just one at a time. And the greatest part of all this was that he realised he could do it from the beautiful, remote part of Iceland that he called home, where his nearest neighbours were miles away. He moved back there and his business is now thriving. He used his already existing knowledge in a way that was less time consuming and more profitable, meaning he also got to spend more time with his family.

It just wouldn't have been possible to reach so many people before the advent and accessibility of the Internet and the social media channels it provides. But money in and of itself is not the goal here. The goal is to create a business model that gives you the time and freedom to actually enjoy the money you earn.

How a Pandemic Showed Us That Diversifying is a Must

In 2020, in the middle of lockdown, I was due to launch my One To Many® programme, and I can honestly say I was extremely worried about it: would people spend money in times of such uncertainty on something that wasn't an essential? Would this be a huge failure?

In fact, my fears were unfounded, and I experienced the most successful launch of my career, making £2.5m in seven days.

As I analysed the results, I began to see why it had been such an epic launch. Yes, I knew my product was great and real value for money, but there was more to it than that. Because it turned out that this was the *perfect* time to be launching a product that focused on making money online. I had been banging on about passive income and diversifying for a couple of years and people had half-heartedly agreed, telling me they'd get to it one day. But suddenly their time was up. They had no business when the offline world shut down.

The lockdown period created more online entrepreneurs than ever before. There was more time for reflection. An unexpected side effect of the almost overnight disappearance of what we had come to know as 'normality' was that millions of us had to find immediate ways to make money. Millions of people whose livelihoods depended on them meeting clients and providing a one-to-one service were now at home all day. Millions who'd had nine-to-five jobs were left wondering if they would have a job to go back to when lockdown was lifted. As a result, ideas started bubbling, different concepts were thought out and, in some cases, radical pivots took place as people pondered: do I really like my job? Could I do something different? What do I really love?

And for plenty of us, this was the perfect time to address those questions and take the first steps to creating a one-to-many product.

The CASsH® System

As I grew my business, created courses and offered advice, I started to realise that I had, almost organically, formulated a step-by-step system for teaching others how to move to a one-to-many business model. I kept teaching it and people kept getting results.

Business isn't complicated; people make it complicated. But not me. I really do like to make things simple – because no one gets excited or inspired by complicated.

And so the CASsH® system was born.

There will be a whole load more detail about the CASsH® system in Chapter 4, where I will break it down so clearly that you'll be implementing everything in no time.

Exercise: Figuring out what your knowledge actually is

Ok, now, this is a nicely designed, well laid out and expertly printed book, so there isn't really much space for you to write in.

However, there will be quite a few exercises (mental, not physical, you'll be pleased to hear) for you to complete as we move through each chapter, so at this point I suggest you get up, stretch your legs, put the kettle on and come back with a notebook and a pen, along with the brew of your choice.

This first exercise needs you to dive into a bit of brainstorming. Here's what I want you to focus on:

What do you know about? What would be your specialist subject on *Mastermind*? Now I guarantee a fair chunk of you who are reading this will be saying, 'I don't know about anything,' but I promise you, there will be something.

To help you out, let's split the answers into three different groups.

1 **Your current business or job** What do you do there? It may be as obvious as the fact that you are an accountant and loads of people struggle with money and understanding the best way to look after it. Or perhaps it is something you have learned from your job that is a standalone skill – say, how to influence people or how to use a certain software program. Maybe you are a manager of a shop, and you have created some amazing systems and processes for providing effective customer service. Or maybe you work in a call centre and have

learned the best way to make sales. Try to think as broadly as you can.

2 **Your previous jobs** Go all the way back. Think about each step of your employment history. Nicola, one of my clients, worked in PR for years and didn't realise how much she could teach to business owners online. She now has a thriving membership for entrepreneurs who want PR.

3 **Your hobbies and your life knowledge** This is often where the gold is hidden. Do you knit? Do you bake? Are you a parent who's worked out how to potty train in a week? *Everything* you have knowledge on should be written down here. Do not overlook anything, no matter how mundane or boring you think it is. I have clients with courses, programmes and downloadables on everything from how to raise confident kids to how to use a camera.

Next, start thinking about whether you could teach someone to do what you do via a course or a programme; or could you teach others to pretty much become you and be your competition (I'll show you why this is a good thing on p. 185)?

Write of all this down and hold on to it – because this could well be your very own 'Dani's napkin!'

CHAPTER 2
Passive and Semi-passive Income Explained

Although at first I wasn't convinced that my early experiences were relevant to this book, I nevertheless started to trawl through my memories in the hope of finding some tales that were worth telling. And I now think it's really important that you understand a bit about me and where I came from, so that you can fully grasp the fact that I am very ordinary.

In the Introduction, I mentioned that I was only twenty-one when I was divorced for the first time. I had been living in a caravan at the chicken farm where I worked. My first foray into adulthood had not given me much of an introduction to the big, bad world (unless the big, bad world consisted of people living in caravans on chicken farms). And then I was single again. With no job, no plan, no home and no experience, other than the Mormon Church, 1980s dance routines and chickens, which I realised added up to a fairly niche skillset.

Regardless, I made a decision that, in hindsight, seems like a combination of bravery, madness and optimism, and

I made up my mind that I was going to move to London. The Big Smoke. Streets paved with gold, opportunities for everyone and all that.

I can remember with clarity the way I felt in those first few weeks – equal parts lost and found. I was adrift in a sea that was unknown to me, trying to steer a course through uncharted waters, which was terrifying. But at the same time, I was untethered, I was free. I was in control and I got to make all the decisions. This was an exciting but also alien concept to me.

First up was finding a place to live, and smartish. I mean smartish as in quickly; not smartish as in a fairly smart place. Because the house I found in an ad and went to have a look around was most certainly not that! But it was available, within my very limited budget and in a commutable location, so I said yes, and moved in immediately, without really giving it a second thought. It was a tiny little box room in a two-bedroom house and I was to live with my landlady.

At first she seemed to be very much your average pensioner. Probably mid-seventies, called me 'lovey' a lot; a pot of tea in a little woolly cosy was more or less a permanent fixture on the living-room table. And all in all, it seemed she would leave me to my own devices, which was fine with me.

However, this assumption was shattered within a few hours of me moving in when I heard a series of grunts and rumblings from below. I could barely imagine what on earth my landlady was up to in her front room.

The sounds reverberated through the house at 5am every day – a rhythmic pattern with just a hint of a melody (I know you're thinking sex dungeon right now, but you'd be wrong). Eventually, curiosity overcame me and I snuck downstairs to see if I could find out what was taking place in this otherwise unremarkable suburban house.

You'll be pleased to hear that what I found out was not at all sinister. Sheila was, in fact, a chanting Buddhist, who also spent a large chunk of her time meditating and practising yoga.

I am aware that today this would be pretty unremarkable, with chanting, meditation and yoga very common in the online coaching world and beyond. But at the time, it was unusual to say the least, especially for an innocent Lincolnshire girl. Although, before I knew it, the chanting became as much part of the scenery as the takeaways in front of Saturday night TV.

What crossed my mind, more and more, the longer I stayed was what a nice, easy way to make cash it was renting out a spare room: you have an empty room, making no money. You fill that room and you make money. The room was already there, and any additional expenses incurred by having a lodger are absolutely minimal.

And there, my friends, is the lesson: the passive income link that you've all been waiting for. And it's an interesting one because, as I said, there are plenty of people who would have you believe that passive income is a new thing or that it doesn't really exist, but this example showed me that it really did – and that it always has.

Now let's move on.

Passive and Semi-passive Income – What's the Difference?

Remember earlier when I said a passive income stream can be defined as 'not trading time for money', well I'm going to caveat that now, as I look at some models where sometimes you will need to invest a little bit of time – otherwise known as semi-passive income.

EARLY DAYS

In the second year of my consulting business, one of my earliest signature programmes was called Fabulous Foundations (we'll call it FF throughout). This is a course for those who want to start making money with an online business. It's a business-basics course, essentially, which goes through all the things I wish I'd known at the start so I could have got here quicker! It includes the following:

- Formulating a marketing plan.
- Setting challenging yet achievable goals.
- Making a sales funnel.
- Simply having confidence in your ability to actually make it happen.

At the time, it consisted of ten modules that I delivered live, and when I first launched it, I was, to be frank, still a bit of a newbie. I wanted to be hands-on with everything I did. This is always crucial to a degree, but back then I wanted to see all the results that my clients were getting, hear first-hand feedback and be there to field enquiries and answer questions directly. It was new and I had to ensure I got it right – to be certain that I was creating the 'know, like, trust' factor (KLT, more of which in Chapter 8) that would lead to long-lasting relationships with my clients.

As such, FF was a classic example of a semi-passive income product. After creating the slides and the workbooks, I then worked an hour each week presenting each module to the people who bought it. Admittedly, an hour a week wasn't a huge impact on my time, but it was still a set amount of time that I had to show up for.

But let's look at this in a different way – a way that I think really underpins the ethos of developing a semi-passive income product.

At the time people laughed at me. They said that I was still having to show up to teach it, so it was hardly passive. So they carried on serving clients in a one-to-one format.

But I could take on a one-to-one client for a charge of £20k for ten hours or work the same hours teaching the FF modules to 100 clients all at the same time, making £150k. Same hours, more money. A success, right? Well yes, of course, especially as this was really the first high-visibility course I had launched.

Learn As You Grow

As my business grew, and I developed and introduced more courses and memberships, I realised that there were further steps I could take with FF. I could keep its value and its content, but now I knew how well it worked, and how it resonated with new business owners, I could take all those learnings and turn it into a fully passive product.

I recorded videos of each module, created an FAQs page and packaged it all together with the online workbooks. Then I marketed it as an evergreen product that could be purchased at any time on my website. An 'evergreen product' is simply a term used for products that are always available for purchase and provide timeless content. It basically means that after you have launched something once, you can remarket it to a customer base that you didn't have during your first launch. It's a great way to maintain a regular income.

FF now generates a recurring revenue stream for me every single month without any further impact on my time. Clients get all the information they need about how to run an online business while working smarter, not harder.

This shows how a very successful semi-passive income product transitioned into an even more successful passive income product. But there are plenty more examples of how a semi-passive model can be a hugely successful revenue-generating system.

DAVID'S STORY

David is known as the Entrepreneurial Dad and he specialises in creating and providing serviced accommodation.

It was March 2020, and the start of a global pandemic. Everything that David had built was starting to take a real hammering. He'd had a successful business to date, but as with all things, a little panic was setting in.

David then signed up to One To Many® and things started to change. He reappraised how he could use his skills in the industry he was an expert in.

Along with his business partner, he'd developed a strategy that had allowed them to thrive in the world of serviced accommodation (basically, short-term rented accommodation), even against the backdrop of lockdowns. He wanted to share it but didn't know where to start. They set about building an audience (I'll be teaching you how to do this in Chapter 5) and then launched a simple, one-off marketing product. They made their first few thousand by sharing their marketing strategies, but they knew that they could create something even better.

They developed a twelve-week programme that made £35,000 in revenue in its first launch. When they launched for a second time, they made over £42,000 in revenue with less effort and less stress because the course was already established.

They helped other people just like them to realise that they could achieve anything they wanted from their property journey.

Since David has been working with me, he has been able to generate over £100k of extra income.

As David himself says, 'It's not simply that it works, but that it works in a way that allows you to stay in integrity and deliver what you were always meant to, being who you are.'

Find out more about David at theentrepreneurialdad.com

Choosing the Right Passive Income Stream for You

Let's cast our minds back to our Buddhist friend, Sheila. Not only did she introduce me to the perils of the cobra and the corpse pose (these are yoga poses and the corpse

– which is essentially when you just lie on the floor – is the only one I excel at), she also opened my eyes to ways of making money that don't require being chained to a desk from sunrise to sunset and beyond.

The first element to bear in mind when looking at which passive income model would work best for you is a simple one.

Cash. Wonga. Capital.

Simply put, some models need money to start off and some don't. Which means some will be more suited to you if you have a bit of cash at your disposal.

Maybe you've just taken voluntary redundancy, have a little nest egg or are saving for a rainy day. (Listen. Do not save for a rainy day. In the UK it rains on approximately 156 days of the year, so you're never going to get rich if you're saving for one of them. If you live in California, I guess your chances are slightly better!) But rainy days aside, having some capital to invest means certain models are available to you.

Let's look at some of them briefly here:

1. BUILDING AN APP

There are plenty of specialists out there who can help you create an app, but it goes without saying that it is the idea for the app itself that will lay the foundations for your success.

The simplest definition of a good app is one that provides a solution to a particular problem.

Much like any business idea, it is hugely unlikely that you will ever come up with something that hasn't been done before. You just need to do it your way.

Don't stress about the coding or any of the techy stuff. Like I said, there are experts out there who specialise in this. What is most important at the outset is that you have an idea that you believe in.

It's usually best to think of a problem that frustrates you. This means you will already be in a better position to offer ideas for resolving the problem.

2. BUILDING A DIRECTORY

People will pay to save time. And if you are that person who can put all the information they need about something in one place, then they will pay you for it. Over and over.

One of my friends, Rachel, did this for the wedding industry. She had a huge directory of all the planners, cake makers, florists, etc. and they all paid to be on her list, so that brides-to-be could then go search for them. Once they were listed, she did nothing more than collect the monthly payment from each supplier.

3. TRADING IN STOCKS/BONDS/CRYPTO

These are open to you if you have experience in trading. **Note:** these options are not without risk because you can lose quickly.

Stocks

Stocks (sometimes known as shares) are units of owner-ship in companies and can give shareholders benefits like dividends and voting rights in company decisions.

The benefit of investing in stocks rather than bonds (below) is that there is a better chance of profit. When companies do well and their financial future looks good, investors buy shares in the hope of making a decent profit. The more people buy, the better the company performs, which could drive up the stock price.

Bonds

Bonds are debt-based investments issued by governments and companies when they need to raise additional capital. In return for loaning money, investors receive regular inter-est repayments and get their initial capital back at a specified time in the future. Bonds are a type of security sold by governments and corporations as a way of raising money from investors. They are typically seen as a safer investment, while stocks usually offer greater opportunity for profit.

Cryptocurrency

Put simply, a cryptocurrency is a new form of digital money. You can transfer your traditional, non-cryptocurrency money like pounds or dollars digitally, but that's not quite the same as how cryptocurrencies work.

If and when cryptocurrencies become mainstream, you may be able to use them to pay for stuff electronically, just like you do with normal money. The biggest plus, and perhaps the strongest indication of their continued success, is that they do away with a lot of the issues around 'real money'. For example, payment systems such as credit cards and wire transfers will be seen as outdated.

YOUR AUDIENCE – WHO ARE THEY?

A key question to ask yourself that will shape your choice of which passive income product to go with is this: do you have an audience? (This could be on Instagram, Facebook, TikTok, YouTube or any other social media channel; or an email/newsletter list, more of which on p. 127.) If so, then courses and memberships are the most sensible route. And there is good news – because building an audience is *the* most important element of creating any kind of membership- or course-based passive income stream, and don't believe anyone who says otherwise. (Statistically, when you launch an online course or membership to your audience the average sign-up is between 1 and 3 per cent. So if you have an audience of 1,000, you can expect anywhere between ten and thirty people to sign up.)

Having said that, I don't really subscribe to these figures as the be all and end all. Because you can have a huge audience, but if that audience is not engaged with your content, then you won't sell anything. Likewise, you can have a small audience of massively supportive and engaged people and sell at way above these averages. (There will be more on this on p. 113.)

Membership groups and courses are my thing. I could write a whole chapter on these two models (oh, wait – there is a whole chapter on these subjects and it's coming up soon!). Suffice for now to say that memberships are successful when done well because we all want to be around like-minded people who share the same interests as us, in a space where we can feel supported and encouraged. And online courses are a never-ending potential income stream that can be used for any, and I mean *any*, type of business.

4. SELL AN EBOOK

If people say to you, 'Can I pick your brain?' about a specific subject, then creating an ebook is a great way to spread your message and generate another revenue stream.

Just think of all the questions you are asked over and over again (or ones that you see asked repeatedly on social media) and remember them – because this is the content that will be gold.

While there are a lot of ebooks out there (remember the Disney lady on p. 14), if you create one that is focused on *what you know your clients want to know*, there will be a market. Also, the good news is that people love reading ebooks on their phones as much as on their computers, so there is additional demand this way.

5. AFFILIATE LINKS

What tools do you use in your business? What books do you read and recommend to your target audience? You could create a page on your website or even a blog that lists affiliate links to each of the things you recommend and then receive payment every time one of your audience buys something through that link.

The Amazon Associates Program is a great example of this. You simply sign up, recommend products to your audience and then earn up to twelve per cent in commission.

6. DROP SHIPPING

Drop shipping is a retail system where you don't keep the products you sell in stock. When you set up as a drop shipping retailer, you buy the item from a third party (a manufacturer, wholesaler or another retailer) who then ships it straight out to your customer.

Drop shipping can be very profitable because the risks are minimal, and it allows you to sell to your customers without the logistical headaches and high running costs that a wholesaler has. All you need is an audience.

7. TEMPLATES

I've worked with many inspirational entrepreneurs who have seized the opportunity to use their knowledge to create a profitable product based on what they already know – information that to them is just a by-product of their 'day job', their interests or their work experience.

My lawyer friend Joanne Fisher realised that all her entrepreneur clients needed legal contracts, but when they were just starting out they couldn't afford to pay a lawyer to draft them, so she made templates they could tweak and sold them on her website. Genius. And a constant stream of income.

You could do this with so many things – order sheets, goal-setting sheets, content-planning sheets, meal plans, fitness plans . . . the opportunities are endless.

The biggest hurdle is recognising that just because *you* know something, that doesn't mean that everyone else does, too. Just remember my definition of an 'expert' – the person who knows the most about a particular subject in an average-sized room – and you won't go too far wrong.

Here are some case studies, so you can get a better understanding of the huge variety of options that are open to you. They are all real people (no names have been changed to protect the innocent), so go check them out. They have all worked with me to develop their specific niches and they are all totally rocking the 'stop-trading-time-for-money' ethos!

NATALIE'S STORY

Natalie had grown her website business quickly but was working entirely in the one-to-one model, with it taking up more and more of her time, leaving fewer hours for her to actually enjoy what she was doing.

She'd reached a ceiling, not just in business and helping the people she wanted to but she knew deep down that if she carried on this way, she would burn out. At the same time, she was really compelled to help the people who couldn't afford the thousands of pounds it would cost to work with her on a one-to-one basis. Yes, there were books, but who would guide them through the processes? After all, having a great website, not a generic one, is so crucial to standing out in your field. And just because someone can't afford thousands shouldn't mean they don't get to do it properly.

This was when Natalie signed up for one of my programmes. I told her she could definitely create a programme for these people at a fraction of her one-to-one cost. At first, she was less than convinced – how could she give them the skills to create their website themselves? How could she help them learn the things she was so used to doing naturally?

But she got smart. She broke down what she did into a process and worked out all the steps. She focused on the programmes and systems that could give people the knowledge of what it really takes, while making it clear, concise and accessible.

This idea eventually became NCDAcademy Wordpress 101, Natalie's signature programme, and it's shown people that even if they're not ready for thousands of pounds' worth of investment, they can still create a website and be seen in the online space.

You can find out more about Natalie at nataliecrowedesigns.com.au

AMANDA'S STORY

Amanda is a photographer who had come to realise that the reason why getting weddings or shoots featured in magazines and blogs used to take such a long time was because each publication had different styles and requirements.

As a result, over the years, to make her life easier she created a spreadsheet with information about each wedding publication – the style of wedding they featured, for example – that would make it more likely that any submission to them would be accepted. She then noticed in wedding groups online that there was information that people would often ask questions about such as, 'Who should I submit this shoot to?' or, 'Does anyone have the contact details for XYZ?' So she created and incorporated all this information in the same easy-to-access place.

Rather than charge her customers, Amanda asked for a £5 donation to Mind, a charity close to her heart.

You can find out more about Amanda at akpbrandingstories.co.uk

SHELLY'S STORY

In April 2021, Shelly created the Jumbo Cake Pack comprised of content she had previously created and sold separately, all bundled together for £15. This included order forms, a how-to-start-a-cake-biz mini course, food-hygiene forms, social media ideas and more. She also then added a little link to a pre-recorded self-study course. In total she made £8,450 just by reusing content she already had.

She also now sells planners, record books, notebooks and journals, all self-published on Amazon, and that has made her over £7,000 in under eighteen months. This has also led her to create a course about self-publishing, which made her £2,500 for five hours' work and which she is now planning to turn into a self-study course.

Both side hustles had no costs and very little initial work.

Find out more about Shelly at shellyshulman.com

The myth of 'You can only succeed if what you're doing is helping people make money'

I am constantly told by people that semi-passive income streams (such as courses and memberships) only work if the area your knowledge is in helps people make money.

This is simply untrue, and I don't want you adopting this mindset. I'm now going to give you two of my biggest success stories from clients – one that has nothing to do with helping people make money and the other that shows you how following the CASsH® system and the steps explained in this book can make you a millionaire, even just from something you love rather than something you know.

LAUREN'S STORY

Lauren wanted to design a membership, but she wasn't sure what it could be about.

After a lot of chatting, Lauren told me that she loved the theatre and acting (she doesn't tell many people, but she was actually in some of the Harry Potter movies as a kid). Well, I told her, just as she liked the theatre, there are others who like it, too, and that's perfect for a membership.

(Remember that people want to be around people who like the same things as them.)

Therefore, Lauren started a theatre membership where members paid a small monthly fee, giving them access to a Facebook group, where they could watch Lauren interviewing West End actors and access theatre tickets at great prices.

During the last couple of years (and even during a pandemic when all theatres were closed) Lauren's membership scheme made her a very healthy revenue of over £2m.

Find out more about Lauren at theatreexpress.co.uk

CAROLINE'S STORY

Caroline is an amazing positive psychology and trauma coach, and a client of mine who was already helping people on a one-to-one basis (women who suffer from trauma from all kinds of things but mainly from narcissistic abuse).

After learning about my CASsH® system, Caroline added courses and memberships to her services and has made £1.7m from them in just a couple of years. More importantly, she has been able to impact a lot more people in this way, which is her ultimate aim.

Find out more about Caroline at carolinestrawson.com

Exercise: Finding out about different models of Passive Income

(If you fancy doing a couple of burpees first then go right ahead, but I'm unlikely to join you!)

To begin, I want you to see what other types of passive or semi-passive income streams you can find and learn about, some of which I've covered in this chapter – but there are plenty more out there. Remember what I said about it not having to be a new thing. And don't think it has to be tech-based either. Think laterally, think creatively and think about the people you know and what they do for a living. You'll be surprised at what you come up with.

When you've delved into the different models in more detail, I want you to research people who have embraced a passive/semi-passive income model successfully. Once you get into this, you will realise just how many there are. Household names, familiar faces, even celebrities who have realised that this is the way to a substantial, consistent income without sacrificing precious time.

Now, taking into account everything you've learned so far, have a think about which model appeals to you the most.

CHAPTER 3
Why Mindset Matters

I'm going to share a flashback.

It's the first day of secondary school and I'm feeling pretty good about it. Out of the whole county, I am one of a handful of kids who got a full scholarship to the most prestigious private school. Safe to say, I am more than a little bit proud of myself.

I'm going to make friends here and do good things.

I sit down at the only table where I know someone. Lucy. She was in my primary school. We've never talked, but at least she is a familiar face.

'Who are you?' says a tall, pretty blonde girl when I sit down.

'Oh, that's Lisa,' Lucy says, before I can speak. 'She's poor.'

Not the introduction I was expecting or hoping for. A table of eight girls stare at me. I turn crimson and want the ground to swallow me up. This was not in the script.

'I'm not,' I stammer.

'She is,' says Lucy. 'She's got a second-hand uniform.'

The girls all snigger and I don't speak again.

At lunchtime, we all queue up, but as I hand over my free-lunch ticket, a small brunette behind me asks, 'What's that?' just loudly enough for everyone to hear and, of course, they all stare.

'It's a lunch ticket,' I answer. I didn't know this was a 'thing' and that I would be the only student who had one.

'Oh! Do you live in a council house?' she asks.

I tell her I don't know. (I genuinely didn't. I asked later that day and discovered we did.)

Later, at afternoon break, I sit in a circle with a group of girls who look much more grown up than me, even though they are in the same year. Lucy is there, too, and I suppose I just want to be around someone I know, even if she was a bit mean.

'You can't sit here,' Lucy says, bluntly. 'We're talking about what cars our parents have and you only have a dad, not a mum.'

'Well, I do actually have a mum,' I reply. 'She just doesn't live with us.'

'What car does your dad have?' says one of the girls.

'He doesn't. He's picking me up on his motorbike,' I say, thinking that must be quite cool. (My world was primarily based on US teen movies in which motorbikes were most definitely cool.)

They all laugh and comment on how they can't believe we exist without a car and how we must be so poor. (My trust in US teen movies is now fading fast.) I'm awkward and uncomfortable but I stay seated. I'll make them like me, I think. I want them to like me. I'll join in and they'll realise I'm nice.

The conversation moves on to middle names and I'm ready for this one. I like my middle name. I'm half Maltese and it's my grandmother's name. So when it comes round to me I tell them proudly, 'My middle name's Carmela'.

'Smella Carmela,' one of them suddenly laughs. 'Because she doesn't have enough money to buy soap.'

And that was the start. The first day of five years of dreading leaving the house. Dreading being picked up my dad who I loved so much. I was Smella Carmela. Either that or simply 'her'.

I was bullied daily, ultimately with a knife to my throat. But that first day at secondary school was the day I realised I was poor. It was the start of all the money mindset issues I would develop further down the line. And I would come to realise, much later in life, that it was not the breaking, but, in fact, the making of me.

Let's Talk Mindset

Yes, mindset. It's at the heart of everything we do – or don't do – and so before we get started on strategy, we need to tackle that brain of yours. I know it's not as interesting as how to make the money, but it makes a massive difference. Trust me. (I'm beginning to sound like a salesperson – but seriously, I mean it: please trust me.)

LIMITING BELIEFS – WHAT ARE THEY, WHY ARE THEY THERE AND HOW CAN YOU DEAL WITH THEM?

Everyone has mindset issues, and usually they're based on one of two things: either a money mindset limiting belief or an imposter-syndrome limiting belief. Some of us have both. It's something I have to continually work at.

Money mindset

This is basically *your attitude to money*.

It's an attitude that lurks in your subconscious – always there, loitering like an unwanted house guest who isn't going anywhere, no matter how often you offer to get them a taxi. Although, the truth is you might not even know it's there.

For instance, when I was growing up, I'd tell everyone who would listen that I was going to be a millionaire, but because of that little money mindset gremlin, I'd actually be thinking, As if! People where I come from don't become rich! I could say it as much as I wanted, but unless I actually believed it, I might as well have been telling people my dad was Mel Gibson.

These little subconscious voices are there all the time and they're the product of all the things we see and hear when we're growing up, or even as adults. And we may not realise they're influencing our thoughts, but they are. We really need to deal with them because they can, and usually will, have a huge effect on how much money we make.

If you can get your head around this concept, you've already taken the first steps to banishing those lurking naysayers from your subconscious.

Mine started working on me when I was eleven on that first day of school but, throughout the years, there have been other experiences that have definitely contributed. Like when I was around thirteen and making up dances in the road with my sister on our estate. (This might seem a bit bizarre but it was totally normal where I lived.) A shiny red Porsche drove past us and I was amazed by it. But immediately the adults around me started jeering. 'Look at that wanker in the Porsche,' one said. 'What a show-off,' said another.

And that sowed a seed into my barely formed subconscious to ensure me of one important fact: *rich people are bad people.*

It's true that I already thought that because of the girls at school who were so mean. But now it was being reinforced, and the problem is that if those thoughts stay with you as you grow up, it doesn't matter how much money you try to make – because deep down there will always be a little voice inside you saying, 'You don't want to make that money! You might get rich and then you'll be the snob in the Porsche and no one will like you. Rich people are bad people!'

Oh, and even if you don't come from a humble background like mine, don't think you've got away with it. Not a chance.

One of my lovely clients, Anna, had been trying to make money in her business for ages. She had all the strategy, but it just wasn't working. I asked her about her money mindset. 'It's fine!' she said. 'I grew up with very rich parents, so money has never been a problem.' But I felt certain something was blocking her, so I probed a bit deeper.

Anna had a two-year-old boy who she adored. In fact, she started her business because she wanted to show him the world. It was when we got to this question that I started to see where the issues might lie: 'What are your early memories of time with your parents?' I asked.

'I never really saw them as they were so busy with their businesses,' she told me. 'But we had an amazing nanny.'

Ah. Ok. And there it was.

It transpired that Anna's gremlin was telling her: 'Making money means you'll have to sacrifice time with your little boy. You can't have both. You'll be a bad parent.'

We worked on this deep-rooted belief (one that she didn't even know she'd had, remember) by looking at where it had showed up in the past, what she was really holding on to and whether there was any evidence to show the belief was true. Sure enough, after working through all this, she started making money a few weeks later and her business is now a great success.

Sandra, another client, needed new branding, but said she just couldn't afford it. I knew that without branding she wouldn't be visible to her ideal client, but even the cheapest branding designer was out of her reach.

A few weeks later, Sandra told me she had £130k in a bank account doing nothing! When I asked her what it was for, she told me her parents had told her to save everything for a rainy day.

So many people I meet are saving for this particular day. Of course, Sandra's parents never told her what this day would look like (after all, as I said earlier, we get hundreds of rainy days in the UK every year – which is the one to spend the money on?), and so she didn't dare spend it. Not even in the knowledge that it would make her more money.

We worked on Sandra's money mindset by looking for patterns in her past that might have contributed to it and writing down some new beliefs, then turning them into affirmations. Once we had done this, she began to invest in branding, and this gave her a tenfold return on her investment in less than a month.

We all need to see money as a positive thing.

And we can't just say it – we need to really believe it. Because what we focus on grows, and there's no way you're going to want to make more of something that you see as bad.

There are so many reasons behind money mindset issues. For example, many of us grew up hearing things like 'Money doesn't grow on trees!' or 'You have to work really hard to get what you want in life'. Phrases such as these have ruined our relationship with money.

I was bankrupt in my early twenties, and hearing a judge telling me 'You are bad with money' led to years of me unknowingly preventing myself from succeeding – because making money had so many negative connotations for me.

But telling yourself you are bad with money is a ready-made excuse and it's going to halt your progress.

You need to realise that there is so much money out there and we don't need to attach emotions to any of it. Not guilt, not shame, not greed. And for those of you who want to focus on helping others, please remember this: helping people and earning money are not mutually exclusive. You can do both.

Once you deal with this mindset stuff, it's all going to become so much easier for you. I did, and my success skyrocketed. I even include a money mindset module in every single programme I do now – that's how important it is.

Imposter syndrome

The second mindset issue I see time and time again is imposter syndrome. This is the voice that tells you: 'Why should they listen to you? You're not the expert. Who do you think you are?'

Yes, you know the one. And I've heard it, too.

Actually, I still hear it every now and again, no matter how many qualifications I get and how many of my clients start making lots of money because of what I teach them. I think it's human nature. We're taught not to brag or think we're special in any way (unless you're a millennial, that is – you guys are *much* better with this one).

But the thing is, it all comes down to what you see an expert as. Remember my definition?

An expert is someone who knows the most about a particular subject in an average-sized room.

Read that again. An average-sized room. Not the world. Not the Internet. Not your town. And believe me, there is definitely something you know more about than anyone else in the room you're in right now. (If you're on your own reading this, go to a coffee shop or any space where there are other people and then ask yourself the same question.)

Another thing to remember is: *your knowledge is not common knowledge.*

To sell as an expert, you need only be a few stages up from where your ideal client is. Put simply, right now, someone, somewhere wants to know what you know. And if they want what's in your head, you can sell it.

Finally, it's worth mentioning that so often what we think of as 'imposter syndrome' could simply be reframed, so that we see it for what it really is: 'they've-been-doing-it-longer-than-I-have syndrome'. But that doesn't mean they know more than you about the subject in question. It just means they may be more proficient at demonstrating that knowledge and understanding the methods, media and tools needed to get it out there.

A great example of this comes from a client of mine called David, who needed a cash injection and wanted to create something quickly that would be a low-cost/multi-client offer. As a joke, one of his friends bet him he couldn't write an ebook about something he knew nothing about within seventy-two hours.

David likes a challenge and he's also brilliant at research. So seventy-two Google hours later he had produced an ebook on how to look after ferrets. His is actually now one of the bestselling books on ferrets and he has a Facebook group of over 6,000 people, in which he sells affiliate products to match. Business is booming.

David has never owned a ferret.

Other limiting beliefs

While money mindset and imposter syndrome are the two biggies focused around money, and the reasons why some people don't seem to be able to make it, there are plenty of other sneaky little limiting, learned and slowly accepted beliefs that can trip us up when we are plotting our paths through the hazardous world of entrepreneurialism. Let's look at a few of them:

- **'But it's all been done before'** We talked about this earlier (see p. 21 and the Brick Lane scenario). Whatever you choose to do, someone else will, in all likelihood, already be doing it. All you need to do is to put your own spin on it, finding a different approach that solves a problem, for example, in a way that is more appealing to your ideal client (who is very likely to be a version of you, BTW). And if no one is already doing it, have a good think about whether it is really a service that will be in demand.
- **Fear of failure** 'I'm not good enough' is something I hear so often, and I've doubtless said it myself a few times over

the years. (For me, in the case of ten-pin bowling or cooking, I was probably right.) But I expect you all remember the old 'But-what-if-I-fall?' quote that is regularly wheeled out by all and sundry? So here's my version of that: *But what if I fall? Well, yeah, you will. Falling is the least of your worries. This isn't Dancing on Ice.* I've had more metaphorical grazed knees than I can count. You fall, you sulk a bit and you get the hell back up and go again. Because these falls are not failures, they are learnings. So you work out why you fell, and you make sure you don't fall for that reason again. *And every time you rise, you become stronger.*

- **Comparisonitis** We all do this. It's nigh on impossible not to in our world of instant social media accessibility. But one thing is for sure: no one has a perfect life, and yes, those pics you see posted by your favourite celeb or business guru have very often been Photoshopped to within an inch of their lives. It's not real – it's filtered, selected and tweaked to create an illusion. So forget the illusions and stop comparing. The only person you have to please is yourself. And remember this at all times: comparisons are always unfair because we are comparing the worst we know about ourselves with the best we presume about others.

- **'I'm not an extrovert'** People believe you have to be the loudest person to be heard. The most 'out there'. The most confident. This is so not true. Plenty of introverts flourish online. Part of me thinks that a big chunk of the problem here lies with the application of personality types in the first place, as demonstrated by a truly enlightening chat I had with my two boys not long ago when I drove them to school. It started with Twin 2, who, out of the blue, said, 'I think I'm an extrovert. But I also think I am an introvert sometimes.' (Apparently, they'd been learning about this at school.) 'You see, that makes me an ambivert, because how I'm feeling or who I'm with makes me act in different ways.' Twin 1 then chimed in with, 'I'm an ambivert, too, definitely.' At first, I thought this all made sense. In fact, I could relate pretty well to this description myself. But I then got to thinking on a broader scale and how keen we are to put people in boxes. To allocate them to a certain group or give them a very specific title. We long for life to be neat. Subconsciously, at least, we decide which category the people we meet fit into and, as was proven by the tentative profiling of two nine-year olds, we decide which group we fall into ourselves. I told the boys that in my opinion we don't need boxes that say 'Extrovert' or 'Ambivert' in the same way that we don't need boxes that say 'Boy' or 'Gay' or 'Religious'. All you need is a box with your name on it. That's who you are. A one-off, mixed bag of weird, creative, funny, sad, irritating, courageous, timid, scared, loud . . . and a million other little bits that make you uniquely you! There is no name required for this precious person other than your own.

Now, going back to the misconception that 'only the extroverts can make money online', you don't need to be put into any box. You get to just be who you are. Forget the boxes and be unapologetic, be bold and, above all, proud to be yourself.

- **Fear of success** I can almost hear you asking, 'Hang on a minute – there's a fear of success as well as a fear of failure?' Well, yes. I'm afraid so. It sits hand in hand with 'fear of getting visible' and is something that I identify with wholeheartedly. There are all sorts of reasons why people are afraid of becoming successful, but one is the genuinely scary prospect of what happens if they then lose it all.

THE DARK SIDE

We are fortunate to live in an age where the world is quite literally at our fingertips. My kids think nothing of FaceTiming friends and relatives in far-flung corners of the globe. I, on the other hand, remember waiting for the pips before pushing my 10p into the slot in a phone box, so, although the Internet is a part of my daily life, it still registers as something extraordinary.

It goes without saying that my business (and millions like it) could not exist without the advent of the Internet, and in particular social media. The opportunities that have been created as a result of this rapid growth of technology are countless. But, as with most things in life, there is a downside. The distance between communicating parties and the ability to make contact while remaining faceless has created a paradise for those keyboard assassins we now know as trolls.

I wish I could write that it's not as bad as it seems, and that it rarely happens, but I can't. And what is also true is that the amount of trolling you experience will increase exponentially with how successful you are.

Speaking from experience, it takes some getting used to, but I'll explain my journey here, as I think it will help.

- **Stage 1** When I first noticed a couple of people pinging off comments, I found it almost amusing; plus, I knew I must be becoming more successful because more people had something to say about me.

- **Stage 2** Things started to get personal: comments about my weight; people saying I'm a liar; others claiming that I'm a fraud. Now, I'm no shrinking violet but it was beginning to hurt.

- **Stage 3** This was a bit of an epiphany and provided me with the one thing I want you all to remember and repeat to yourselves like a mantra if you start to get any online grief: *you'll never find someone trolling you who is doing better than you are.* It's simple and 100 per cent true! No one who is a success has the time to consistently attack another person (and if they do, think how much more successful they could be if they ploughed the same effort into actually developing their own business).

I was persecuted, victimised, singled out and blatantly bullied by a group of people in my industry quite early on in my career. Unlike the usual faceless online bullies, these were respected and well-known people. For some misguided reason, they had a vendetta against me and ganged up to spread their word and try to harm both my business and me as a person.

They said really mean, hateful – and totally untrue – stuff, and a big chunk of me was thinking, Is it worth it? Should I get a normal job again? I really don't need this crap.

But then the real me – the one who fiercely believes in justice; the one who will not put up and shut up – thought simply, No. These are lies. I'm not taking it.

I'm going to choose the other path. Do I want to cave in or do I want to create an extraordinary life for me and my family?

So yes, there is a dark side. But always remember the cause of most, if not all, negative comments about you or what you are doing will be jealousy.

Suffice to say, I stopped them lying (by going legal). I focused on me. I let the trolls fester in their little world of bitterness and spite. And I made over £2m from my next launch.

As Frank Sinatra once said: *'The best revenge is massive success.'*

Anxiety in Business

Dealing with anxiety as an entrepreneur is a major challenge at the best of times. But sticking to some simple, self-governed rules can make a huge difference here, with no major impact on time, no massive learning required. Just an ability to reflect and be self-aware when the signs start to make themselves visible.

Be honest with yourself and remember what American TV journalist Bob Schieffer said: 'Once you realise that there is life after mistakes, you gain a self-confidence that never goes away'.

UNDERSTAND YOUR TRIGGERS

You know that 'Unfollow' button? Or if you're not feeling quite so brave, how about the one that says 'Mute'? Use them. Tell your staff and your friends that you do not have any need to know the day-to-day activities of whoever or whatever your trigger may be.

> **If they have no impact on your productivity, they do not need to feature in your life.**

SLOW DOWN AND BREATHE

This applies both literally and metaphorically. The more 'woo' the world becomes, the more useful 'everyday, normal' breathwork, meditation and mindfulness become. To begin, just sitting still for five minutes in a quiet environment can be hugely beneficial. Also, slow down your reactions: take a beat to reflect before you react, and only then respond. Hold off on pressing 'Send' on that potentially contentious email and revisit it a couple of hours later to see if your tone conveys precisely the message you want to get across, or if your state of mind at the time of writing impacted your intended tone of voice.

DON'T SWEAT THE SMALL STUFF

It's human nature to latch on to the little things that we have more chance of controlling when the big stuff is gathering around us ominously. But the way you manage the bigger picture is what will set you apart from your competitors, and, despite any initial concerns, addressing and resolving these more challenging issues will have a far bigger impact on your mindset and your day-to-day mental wellbeing than ticking off a few mundane tasks that have no bearing on your success, productivity or satisfaction.

INDULGE IN SOME 'POSITIVE PROCRASTINATION'

Take a break, but don't spend it mindlessly scrolling through social media, where you are very likely to accidentally come across one of the previously mentioned, avoid-at-all-costs triggers.

Do the thing you've wanted to do for weeks. Go for that walk. Watch the next episode of the Netflix escapist teen drama you love. Buy those shoes. The time out will help you hugely and you will not come back feeling like you have 'wasted' that time.

Motivation

Maintain your belief, maintain your vision and maintain your dignity.

Let's just talk motivation now. And my biggest advice on this subject is simple: *don't believe the hype!*

So many online personalities sell the story that they are always motivated, always on it, always feeling it. That's great – really, it is; but I'm sorry (not sorry) – I don't buy it.

We all have our moments when it gets tough, when inspiration runs dry, when our mojo is MIA. But it is how we react to these moments that separates those who consistently achieve from those who consistently fail.

Which is why I just want to talk a little bit about finding your bigger purpose and loving and nurturing and cherishing it – because this is what will sustain your motivation and enthusiasm for what you do.

This is an interesting section for me to write, because up until quite recently, I would have confidently said that my only purpose was to prove the bullies wrong by making a sh*t ton of cash and living an amazing life. However, in keeping with the 100-per-cent-honesty policy within the pages of this book, I want to share a story from the recent past rather than from the depths of my memory bank.

MY PURPOSE

I was at a swanky hotel, taking part in a retreat for seven-figure entrepreneurs (business owners who have made more than £1m). Everyone was being asked what their bigger purpose was and, unsurprisingly, I was heavily involved in helping the other attendees work out theirs. Once we'd been round the table, there was just me left, so I gave the usual answer (that I didn't have a bigger purpose than making money), adding something along the lines of 'I'm tired of everyone coming up with these holier-than-thou statements. Why can't mine just be to make money? Why does it always have to be the old, "Ooh, I want to change the world and enable fifteen million women to step into their own power and harness their transformative inner essence!"'

This caused plenty of chuckles, but as I thought back to what I had said throughout the day, and what my fellow masterminders had said, something started to emerge.

Maybe I *did* have a bigger purpose. No, scratch that. I *definitely did* have a bigger purpose. I just had to reframe everything I had already said to encapsulate it in a statement that exactly reflected how I wanted it to look. And this was it:

My purpose is to help others who are passionate about changing the world to change the world.

I don't need or want to change the world. But plenty of my clients do. Therefore, I am their facilitator for change. Their conduit for growth. Their guide on their very own world-changing journey.

And that suits me just fine!

All limiting beliefs are learned behaviours. Therefore, it stands to reason that you can also learn how to overcome what limits you. And I can, and will, help you. Your knowledge, experience and expertise, on the other hand, are your very own superpowers.

Exercise: How to create a more positive money mindset

1   WORK OUT YOUR MONEY STORY

Once you know what this is, you can begin to look at the patterns you might be repeating and why that might be. Grab a journal/notebook/tablet and try to answer the following questions:

- What is your earliest memory of money? (Mine is my parents arguing over it. You can see how that might have instilled some negativity about money.)
- What other memories have shaped your view of money over the years, as a child and a young adult? (This can sometimes be emotional, so be prepared for it.)
- Finish this sentence: 'Money is . . .' **Note:** if you have finished the sentence with something negative, write down the opposite of that statement on a Post-it note and stick it somewhere you'll see it every day. (Mine was 'Money is evil'. Crikey.)

2   EXPLORE WHAT YOU THINK ABOUT PEOPLE WITH MONEY

- What do they look like?
- Where do they live?
- How do they act?
- Do they look like you?

This will identify any unconscious bias you hold about who people with money really are. I thought multi-millionaires were all on TV. I certainly didn't think they looked anything like me – and now I am one! The thing that helps with this part is googling and getting to know others who come from similar backgrounds to you who have money now (it certainly helped me). This makes you realise it's totally achievable.

3   HONESTY AND AWARENESS

Now let's get real about the money you have now. As I said earlier, whatever we focus on grows – so if we hide from our bank statements, we're not going to attract more money.

You need to know exactly what your money situation is, regardless of whether it's good or bad. (And remember, no meanings or emotion should be attached to money – try thinking of it as tokens at a fairground.) Once you know how much money you do or don't have, it's much easier to know what you want or need to bring in. So take the time to go through your bank statements in detail. Work out what comes in and what goes out. Do not get all ostrich about any of it.

4   BIGGER PURPOSE

Now let's try to work out your bigger purpose. Ask yourself these questions:

- Why do you want success?
- Who are you doing it all for?
- What legacy would you like to leave?
- What would you like to change in the world?

CHAPTER 4
Online Memberships and Courses

I tried to get involved in a few clubs when I was a kid. Maybe 'tried' is a bit misleading. 'Coerced' may be a better word. I think I was tricky to guide in a specific direction because I wasn't what was thought of as a 'typical child'. (**Note:** I wasn't very far into my parenting journey when I realised that this does not exist!)

I wasn't particularly sporty as a child. I think I wanted to be a performer of some kind, but where I came from, the only chance of that happening was on stage at Butlin's Skegness singing 'Wake Me Up Before You Go-Go' to an assortment of bemused holidaymakers. (Yes, that happened.) In hindsight, one of those cafés with self-deprecating names like Geek Retreat, where people sit around playing Dungeons and Dragons (or whatever the current version of this is) would have suited me just fine. But I'm pretty sure they weren't a thing in 90s Lincolnshire.

I do remember there were two groups that I had brief dalliances with, though. First off was the time-honoured go-to for any girl; traditional, wholesome fun and educational, too. Yep, I was enlisted as a Brownie. What could possibly go wrong?

Well. As you've doubtless come to realise, I'm not now, nor have I ever been, someone who understands the attraction of spending the night in a damp tent. Especially not the tents the Brownies used in those days, which looked very much like something from *The Greatest Showman*. But amazingly, this is not the reason why my Brownie membership was what can only be described as short-lived.

My dad was contacted by the leader – the 'Brown Owl' – and asked to pop in for a chat. The upshot was that they considered me to be what in the adult world would be known as 'too opinionated'. To be honest, it's a fair cop. One thing that is guaranteed to wind me up is being made to do something I don't think is a good idea. No wonder, then, that when the Brown Owl told us all to form a human pyramid or create a nice collection of leaves, I would have raised my objections against such inane and unnecessary activities.

I made such objections on numerous occasions, leading to the suggestion that I may be better suited to some other weeknight activity. Looking back, as we now strive to produce confident, articulate and strong young women, it strikes me that the Brownies missed out on an opportunity to shape my personality and, perhaps, revolutionise the rest of my childhood and even my life. Alas, they did not see it that way, so I found myself seeking out another club to join.

Enter ballet. Surely there was no trouble that an opinionated and slightly-lacking-in-social-skills eight-year-old could cause while decked out in a tutu?

Well, yes. And no. I didn't really get to do any talking because, well, it was a ballet class, but that didn't mean my presence in the room was a welcome one.

After a couple of weeks, my dad received another of those phone calls: 'Could you pop in for a chat, please?'

And it went something like this:

'Ah, Mr Vassallo, thanks for coming in,' said the teacher. 'We just need to have a little chat about Lisa. While her enthusiasm for dancing is, it must be said, commendable, her ability to follow, let alone master, any of the moves is, on the other hand, not so impressive.'

'Stop being such a snob, let her have a chance,' (or something along those lines) was my dad's response. Which led the conversation from that point away from the realms of politeness and tact, culminating in these words from the teacher (which I believe to be verbatim): 'Your daughter has all the dance ability and grace of a baby elephant.'

No more pliés for me, then.

And onwards through my less-than-idyllic childhood years, moving seamlessly into my turbulent teenage years. Unsurprisingly, my opinion of organised communities of any sort remained unenthusiastic. In my eyes, they were too rigid in their rules, too unwilling to entertain discussion and too closely related to enforced fun (something that back then, and still today, I am not an active participant in).

If this was an 80s film, we'd now have a fast-forward-a-few-years segment involving some pretty flaky technology showing me at various stages of my journey into adulthood. But as this is a book, I'll just plop in some words and you can do the visuals in your heads. Here goes.

Marriage number 1. To a chicken farmer. Divorce. Move to London. Get a job. Get a better job. Long hours. Candle burned at both ends. Marriage number 2. Pregnant very soon after. Twins. Panic. Divorce.

That just about covers it. And now for a bit more detail.

The twins.

I hadn't planned on becoming a mum to one bouncing baby so soon, let alone two. But in keeping with my decision making in life as whole, I don't hang about!

Firstly, I knew immediately in my gut that my days of working all hours in the City would need to come to an end. Not just from a logistical point of view (I'm talking practicalities, health and stamina to name but three), but from an 'I-want-to-be-a-decent-mum-who-is-there-for-her-kids' perspective, too. (If only there was a way to work fewer hours and earn more money. Someone should write a book about that . . .)

After five months of kidding myself that these two new small humans were going to have to just fit into my life, I handed in my notice at my investment-banking job, feeling a little bit gutted as I'd worked hard to get where I was. I decided to take a job nearer to home so I could at least parent them before and after work.

But I had no idea what to do – like, what to actually *do* now – or how having twins would play out. I was a confused mess. A patchwork of excited, terrified, nervous, shocked and intimidated.

I didn't know anyone who had had a multiple birth, and while all my friends who'd had kids were offering advice, I kind of knew that I needed to speak to women who had given birth to more than one baby at the same time.

So I did what everyone does when they want advice about everything from setting the temperature on their thermostat to checking the best way to remove a wine stain – I googled it.

That opened up a whole new world that I was not aware existed. And unbeknown to me, I had just taken my first tentative steps on the journey that would eventually lead me to where I am now. Because, ladies and gentlemen, I had discovered the world of online groups and memberships!

Who knew there were thousands of women like me who wanted support with their impending multiple births? I discovered that there were loads of friendly, welcoming and information-packed groups where I could find out anything (and I mean *anything*) that I needed to know: what's the best car seat? How do I feed them? When will I sleep? Dealing with the after-effects of a C-section. What the heck is a bassinet?

Just being surrounded by women in the same boat as me, I immediately felt supported. My questions no longer seemed silly. And this brought something home to me that would never be far from my mind as my journey continued:

Never underestimate the power of community.

Let's be clear. I was still somewhat terrified about the arrival of two small people who would rely on me to keep them alive. But I now knew I was not the only one who felt like this. I could access practical and emotional help, and, perhaps even more importantly, I could just vent and there would always be someone to chat with.

Looking back, I realise that the reason I very quickly felt at home in this kind of support network is because of my aforementioned dislike of enforced fun. I really don't like groups with a weekly meet-up time, and before-and-after chatting with other members. It's just not me. But this way I could come in and out at times that suited me and get the specific info I needed. (And while becoming pregnant with twins might seem like a slightly unconventional route to learning the underlying principles of the business I would build, you've probably come to realise that I rarely go about things in the traditional way, so I think it kind of fits well.)

The first seed had been sown, and while it would grow somewhat slower than the soon-to-arrive small people, it would, none the less, grow.

How to Develop Online Memberships and Courses

I mentioned earlier that I could write a whole chapter about these two models, and, as I always keep my word, here it is.

> There can be no dispute that serving one to many is the quickest way to make passive income.

But so many people seem to struggle with believing they can do it; or, just as often, they think it's some kind of dodgy, unscrupulous, get-rich-quick scheme.

There are two things to remember:

1 Only you decide what your scruples are.

2 You won't get rich quick, I'm afraid. There is plenty of
   work to be done before you'll be counting your profits.
   The only overnight success I've had is getting more than
   five hours' sleep!

It was the introduction of the readily accessible world as
provided by the Internet that set the ball rolling. People
started to realise that they could learn from others, which
got them thinking: Why couldn't I do that? Or, That guy is
getting thousands of clicks showing us how to replace the
filter in the tumble dryer – why can't I share my
knowledge?

Lightbulbs lit up and cogs clicked into place as millions
of people around the world realised that the people they
were watching were really only a couple of steps away from
them and what they knew. We all know different things.
Think about it. Think about your current job, your previous
job, your hobbies, your interests . . .

> ### You know stuff! And if you know stuff, you can sell that knowledge.

Once you realise and appreciate what you already know,
the next question is how to sell it?

Now, before the world shrank to the small device in
your hands or on your desk, sharing that knowledge
would've been a major challenge. Let's just go back to
the distant past: a time when a mobile phone meant an
extra-long curly cable on the landline and doing your
homework meant going to the library. We're talking BTI
(Before The Internet). Back then, you'd have been going
to meetings in a village hall once a week, subscribing to a

postal newsletter or relying on ads in the local paper. Suddenly, Ben in Alabama's expertise on dog training or Helen in Munich's encyclopaedic knowledge on fossil collecting became your lifeline. For just a few quid a week.

Online training can basically be summed up as:

- **Programmes** Where you teach your knowledge live online for a specific period of time. Let's say, for example, a six-week course for couples on how to plan their wedding. The information is usually drip-fed, like in the old days, when we would have had to wait for next week's episode in a TV series.
- **Courses** Usually a more passive version of a programme. The learnings might be recorded videos or they might just be workbooks and people are more likely to be able to complete the course whenever they like.
- **Memberships** You might have a Facebook group to chat to other people planning their wedding and there might be guests who come in to teach people how to arrange the flowers or the etiquette when Aunt Jane (who you've met just once) wants to invite her twenty closest friends. It's less learning, more hanging out with like-minded people. The big advantage here? If you're tired of the online cliques, you can start your own club. (No one's going to tell you you're not allowed in then!)
- **Workshops or masterclasses** Usually a one-off class online for an hour or maybe two, covering one subject. Using our wedding example again, it could be 'What You'll Need to Plan for your Wedding and When'. You can use audio, video, workbooks, live recorded sessions,

tasks, activities. You choose what you work best with and what you are most comfortable with.

As I will explain, there are certain elements of creating a successful online space that I believe are absolutely compulsory. But in essence, it just needs to package up all your knowledge in a lovely, user-friendly bundle that your ideal clients (more on these peeps on p. 90) will be able to learn from while enjoying themselves at the same time.

In my first year as a business coach, I made around £220k. Pretty good, right? That was over five times my annual salary in my 'normal' job. But – and this is a big but:

I was working on average eighty-hour weeks to make this amount of money.

Yep. I still wasn't spending enough time with my twins. I'd traded a nine-to-five job to work from 6am to 10pm instead. This was not the self-employed life I had imagined. However...

...one year later, I was making over £1m per year and working, on average, thirty hours a month.

And this was because I'd come to realise I was teaching each of my one-to-one clients the same things. Of course, there were specifics that related only to them, but the fundamentals were always the same. I had developed steps, stages and strategies to simplify their route from time-starved stress heads to productivity pros.

So I did the sensible thing. I wrote it all down, packaged it up and it now underpins my teachings in all my groups and programmes, but in particular my flagship product One To Many®. Because, put simply, it's a lot more profitable to teach 100 people the same thing at the same time than to do it individually.

The CASsH® System and How to Use It

Before we go any further, let me stress two things:

Firstly, *I'm nothing special*. But I did go from £30k debt to turning over seven-figure sums annually within the space of three years, so what I am is actual, living proof that it can be done.

And secondly, *'I'm not a f*cking magic fairy!'* I can't magic-ally make a million pounds appear in your bank account. You are going to have to implement the things I am telling you here.

These two things are well worth remembering. It's like buying a posh pair of trainers from Nike for £200 and then moaning that you're not running any faster after two weeks of wearing them. You need to put in the work. It's a simple equation:

Learn the steps + follow the steps = success

But what *are* the steps? I hear you ask.

Well, I coach my clients using the CASsH® system I mentioned earlier – it's a blueprint that has worked for all my semi-passive income streams and for my clients'. (And before you all scream, 'But Lisa, there are two Ss in it!' I know, I know, I know! But please cut me some slack here and allow me some creativity! It still sounds like CASH when you say it, so we can all ignore that other little s right?)

Now. Let me talk you through what it actually means, then – because hidden within the snazzy acronym are the fundamental steps you need to take.

C IS FOR CLIENT

Before you consider what you want your passive income product to be, it is imperative that you work out the client you want to serve. You have to know them inside out. Keep that in mind as we go through the rest of the sections, as very soon we will be focusing in detail on defining and attracting your ideal client. Instead of thinking, I want a membership or, I'll have a course, think instead: Who are the people I want to help? Once you know that, they'll tell you what they want.

A IS FOR AUDIENCE

Once you know your ideal client, you can start growing an audience of those people. To do this, it is crucial that you know where your ideal client hangs out. After all, you wouldn't advertise for Gucci in Primark or vice versa.

I decided right at the beginning that Facebook was where my audience would mainly be found. I started a group and used video as my primary resource, because, well, I like being in front of a camera. But because I had done the legwork and figured this out, I grew an audience of 1,500 of my ideal clients in five months, giving me a six-figure income really quickly.

Also, it's so important to nurture that audience.

What I mean by that is you can't just grow an audience on Facebook and Instagram, for example, and then leave them there until you're ready to sell them something. You need to keep them warm.

Think of it like this: say you're at a bar and a stranger comes up to you and says, 'Fancy coming back to my place?' You're likely to say no and probably think they're a bit of a dick. But if every time you went to that bar, that same person took the time to get to know you, have a bit of a chat and then, after a few weeks, they asked you back to their place, you'd be a lot more likely to say yes.

It's exactly the same with your audience. You can't just leave them there and only chat when you want them to buy something. Don't be the dick at the bar.

Bear this in mind as you grow an audience in whatever social media platform you choose. I would strongly recommend sticking to one or maybe two and using a sales funnel to grow a list of interested people, who will get to know, like and trust you. (Don't worry, I'll explain what a sales funnel is in Chapter 6, where I'll go into growing your audience in more detail.)

S IS FOR STRUCTURE AND SYSTEMS

Once you get some feedback from your audience on what they would love you to create for them, you're ready to work out which type of passive income stream you want to sell.

The fun bit starts then, as you can begin thinking about where you'll host it, getting the tech ready and starting to work out the structure.

Will you use video, workbooks, etc.? What do you enjoy doing? Use that as your medium.

TOP TIP

Don't think everything you do has to be super professional every time. I've sold courses just filming twenty-minute tutorials on my iPhone or using Zoom. When you feel inspired, just go for it. People will like (and therefore trust) you a lot more if you are relatable. Do not give yourself the excuse of needing a load of professional equipment and software to sell your knowledge. You don't.

Remember: progress over perfection.

THE SECOND S IS FOR SELLING

Yes, you are ultimately here to sell your product and create a sustainable, profitable business, regardless of what you actually 'do'.

Selling online is called launching and there are lots of different ways to do this: masterclasses, video series, challenges and all sorts. All of which can be fun. We'll cover all this and more in Chapter 8.

BIG TIP ALERT

Sell Before You Create!

I am a big believer in selling something before you create it. This means not writing an entire course in full initially, but rather bullet pointing what will be in it so that you can put the facts on to a sales page. When enough people buy in, then you can write the whole course, knowing it's not going to be a waste as people have paid for it already. I know this seems cack-handed, and a bit scary, but honestly, it's a great way of testing. I've seen so many people spend months creating a product, get all excited, then get it out there and nobody buys it. There is no better incentive to creating that course than knowing people have already paid you for it. If this terrifies you, you could always write the first module.

H IS FOR HAPPY

Ah, who wouldn't love this one?

Bottom line is: you need to think about how to keep your lovely clients happy, so that they stay with you in your membership group or buy more of your courses, and are there, ready for you to re-market to them.

You're probably thinking right now that this 'passive' income is not very passive at first! You're growing an audience, you're creating content, you're learning how to launch stuff. But it does become passive the second, third, fourth and all the subsequent times that you sell it because by then it's all written and all the marketing for it is in place.

However, you won't get to those second and third times unless the clients you sell it to the first time are happy. They are the ones who will shout about how good your offering was, so that you won't have to spend money on advertising. (Because of a bad experience early on with Facebook ads, I didn't use any more until I'd made seven figures – and I didn't really need to either, because my clients shouted about how good my programme was.)

Plus, happy clients will buy other stuff from you. And it is much cheaper to sell to an existing client than to find new ones through advertising.

Who Do You Want to Sell To? (And Why Is It Important to Get This Bit Right?)

I'm just going to drop this. No explanation. No background. No introduction. Because before we go any further with this chapter, I want you to have this imprinted in your mind. Make it your mantra. Print it out on a piece of paper and stick it on your desk. Get it tattooed on your arm. Seriously, it is *that* important and I never, ever want you to forget it:

Create a mindset that says, 'I will work with the right clients, not all the clients'.

I understand that when you are just starting out, it's natural to want to sell to everybody. Surely getting as many clients as possible is best? They'll all give you the cash, right? And what could be more important than that? Well, heads up: this is the first big mistake you will make, and I am talking from experience.

Let's go back a few years to when I started my wedding-planning business. I got a shiny, new logo and a website, printed a few business cards and I was ready to go. Next, I booked in at some wedding fairs and prepared to welcome all the lovely couples who would be throwing themselves at me, begging me to plan their weddings for them.

Well. That's not quite what happened, but after some more wedding fairs and a bit of word of mouth, a few couples did book me, and I set about planning their nuptials.

To begin with, I was just so excited to have some customers that I didn't really give a thought to the type of weddings they were looking for. I also (and this causes me physical pain to write now) reduced my prices if they said they couldn't afford me. Which makes this a suitable time to post the next mantra you will need at all times:

If your ideal client cannot afford to pay you, they are not your ideal client.

Back then, of course, I didn't know *what* an ideal client was, let alone *who*, so I went ahead planning weddings in village halls, marquees, rambling country hotels and anywhere my couples would pay me to work.

And guess what? No matter how busy I got, I just wasn't feeling it and the couples would always choose whoever was the cheapest rather than the right one for them. This wasn't me, and these people, lovely though they usually were, weren't the people I wanted to work with. But the burning question remained: who *did* I want to work with?

As is usually the case, I started to realise that my ideal client was a version of me. Ok, I'll admit it, a slightly cooler, younger and more stylish version, but none the less, I was in there somewhere.

I wanted to plan cool, urban, stripped-back, absolutely-not-a-chair-cover-in-sight weddings. To use a phrase that I coined at the time: 'urban-luxe' weddings.

So. I stopped. I rebranded. I targeted just the couples who wanted the kind of weddings I wanted to create. And, in doing so, I alienated myself from 95 per cent of all the couples out there.

But. And again, this is a huge but.

The remaining 5 per cent all came to me. And none asked for a discount or bought solely based on price.

I niched down just about as far as I could go, because, as any Americans among you would say: *the riches are in the niches.* (**Note**: I realise that this doesn't quite work for all those who say 'neesh' rather than 'nitch', but hopefully, you get the idea.)

That's what I did. But how? Which brings us back to . . .

. . . WHAT IS AN IDEAL CLIENT AND HOW DO YOU FIND THEM?

Let's start with another message you need to keep at the forefront of your mind at every stage of defining, attracting and, ultimately, securing your ideal client. (Yes, I know there have been a few of these but getting this bit right underpins every single thing you do in making your online business a success.)

Finding your ideal client is not doing market research.

We are taught in business to find a gap in the market and then sell to those people. This is called doing your market research. However, I don't believe that's the best way. I believe finding your ideal client is the way to a successful business that you find joy in.

And you need to think: if someone was to walk through your door and said they wanted to work with you, who would you want them to be? (Ok, you may not have an actual door, but let's stick with the analogy anyway!)

It's about getting clear on who you want to work with rather than who wants to work with you. If you have worked out who your ideal client is – created a brand that resonates with them, a service that aligns with their values and a personality that appeals to them – they will choose to work with you because of these things, and not because of price.

Going back to my wedding business, we weren't cheap – far from it, in fact – but we were unique. And because we had nailed our ideal client, people would phone up and say, 'We are booking you' before they'd even heard our prices.

We put our prices up three times in a year and it made no difference. We still got clients.

GETTING CLEAR ON YOUR MESSAGE

Once you have identified your ideal client (get those pens ready because of course there is an exercise coming to help you with this – see p. 97), you will find it much easier to decide on your strategy to make yourself irresistible to them.

Let's say you have a stinker of a toothache. You rush to the chemist to get something to help you and on the shelves there are five products to choose from. Four of them cost around £1 and their branding says something like, 'Gets rid of pain quickly'. The fifth costs £10, but the label says, 'Guaranteed to eradicate tooth pain within ten minutes'. Most likely, you'd plump for that one every time.

Likewise, you must clearly and concisely advertise what you do and how you do it in a way that will get the attention of who you do it for. Once you have their attention, the real work starts. You must represent your ideal client in everything you do and say; there has to be consistency in your branding, your values, your voice and your personality.

- You'll need to be clear on **what your value is**. What problem are you solving for them? How will what you do improve their lives? Once you know this, and how to share this 'too-good-to-refuse' offer, it's all about sharing it in your content.
- Your **brand should be clear and strong**. It should reflect your values, as well as creating a style that suits your

image and will be right up the street of the client you're trying to target.

- Think about **the demographic of your ideal client and what would appeal to them.** Nothing can be overlooked when it comes to attracting them.
- Make sure that you are **sending out a clear message** that is targeted only at your ideal client. If they are all about sustainability, don't use a pic of you drinking through a straw on your website. If they are into cool cocktail bars, don't hold your client meetings in a Wetherspoons. And if they are lovers of literature, make sure all the copy on your site flows like a thing of beauty.
- You need to sound as if you are **speaking to them directly.** Get your voice, your tone and your cultural references right. The more these resonate with your ideal client and make them feel like they're having a chat rather than being sold to, the more likely they will be to engage and, ultimately, buy from you.

Jeff Bezos once said, 'Your brand is what people say about you when you aren't in the room.' This is so true. It's all about how people think of you and your offers and how you make them feel, too. So forget thinking about branding in terms of colours or fonts, logos and websites. I had no website at all until I was making hundreds of thousands. A website and logo are nice to have, but not essential. A brand is not. I cannot overstate how important all this stuff is. It is a massive game changer.

Another great thing to remember is this:

You simply cannot be too niche.

So let's have a look at some clients of mine and how they have niched their businesses. These amazing people have taken their knowledge, skills and experience and specialised within their area of expertise to attract and engage with a super-specific audience, with incredible results.

MATT'S STORY

Matt Boyles is the founder and CEO of Fitter Confident You. After nine years in marketing, liking but not loving it, Matt discovered the world of fitness and trained and qualified as a personal trainer, making the classic wet-behind-the-ears mistake of saying he would train anyone.

As you now know, the problem with that is your ideal client doesn't know that you are speaking directly to them – and they need to know that you are, otherwise you fall through the cracks.

The biggest irony of Matt's story was that he left a marketing career to work in the fitness industry, but in doing so he instantly forgot everything he'd learned along the way.

As a PT, training people in the parks of London, Matt put himself out there enough to generate a trickle of enquiries and to keep himself going. He met and got to work with some lovely people, but in his own words, he 'wasn't doing anything earth-shattering'. He was a regular PT, doing regular PT work with a regular number of clients and a regular income. Which was all fine. But he had an inkling he could be doing more.

By the end of 2017, he was well aware of the big online personal trainers, and an idea started to form: maybe he could do that, but better. He could bring in more elements – meditation, confidence, group support – all of which were a step up. But it was when he was reflecting on his own journey that the real lightbulb moment occurred.

Growing up gay and not into rugby or football, Matt had mostly felt left out of fitness and sport, believing it was what other people did. However, from his mid-twenties onwards he started to discover the power of fitness, nutrition and a regular routine, all of which helped to build his inner strength, confidence and self-esteem.

Anxiety and depression are usually higher in almost all minority groups, and, knowing first-hand the benefits of finding his rhythm with working out, Matt realised there was a whole world of gay, bi, trans and queer guys out there who felt like he used to. So he took the decision to stand up and be counted, and his mission came into focus: to help his community build confidence, strength and fitness on their own terms.

Business-wise, the results were incredible. He really wanted to be able to stop his face-to-face training at some point, and that happened just eight months after starting Fitter Confident You, his online PT programme.

Matt's words summarise his story, and the power of niching, perfectly: 'Personally, I've never felt so fulfilled and connected to who I am and what I do. I have a purpose. I've built a tribe. And I'm so proud every single day of what I do and how I get to reach, support and encourage my community.'

You can find out more about Matt at fitteryou.net

FLISS'S STORY

In the middle of the 2020 lockdown, like so many other entrepreneurs, Fliss decided that she need to pivot her business. She needed to tweak and niche down her veterinary physiotherapy business from seeing and treating clients one-to-one to an online service. There were two main reasons for this:

- The pandemic meant that she couldn't see anyone in person.
- The birth of her second child meant she wanted a more flexible, sustainable business arm.

As a qualified veterinary physiotherapist, Fliss had noticed a lack of online resources for her sector, so she decided to use her knowledge to create a course to teach other vet professionals rehab skills to incorporate into their current practices.

She launched this the first time round and had only three students. Then she discovered me, and my One To Many® (OTM) programme, and realised it was exactly what she needed. Eight weeks into the OTM course, she launched again, and the number of students on her course increased to thirteen.

Alongside this, using a strategy she had learned in OTM she launched a membership, providing monthly CPD (continuing professional development) to already-qualified vet physios, bringing in a guest speaker each month.

As a direct result of these two new income streams, she increased her revenue by 50 per cent, going from a profit of £43k to one of £89k!

The best thing for Fliss is that her business model fits in around her family. She now works two hours a day in the evenings on her online business and two full days with one-to-one clients.

Fliss has started enrolling students for her next intake and she is fully booked, with people signing up for the next two years.

Find out more about Fliss at thesmallanimal-rehab.com

Exercise: How to identify, then find your ideal client

It's time to consider who you want to help so you can start the CASsH® system and begin growing an audience of those people.

1 Think hard about who you want to work with and get to know them.

2 Next, try to write fifty sentences about them. For example: she shops at Waitrose. She is passionate about the environment. She has children.

3 Now think about where that ideal client hangs out. Which social media platforms do you need to be posting content on?

4 Lastly, think about your own values. What do *you* care about? Which five words might sum you up? These will be important when you're attracting your ideal client.

CHAPTER 5
Growing an Engaged Online Audience

Twins, then.

Two tiny, non-stop whirlwinds of noise, chaos and never-ending bodily fluids. And what do you know? My up-until-this-point dormant maternal side kicks in in an overwhelming torrent of love and pure amazement that I've created something as perfect as these two tiny individuals.

I immediately loved the twins unconditionally and completely, but I also knew I wasn't going to be a full-time, stay-at-home mum for long. It works for a lot of people, but it just wasn't who I was. I tried a baby club once and felt so uncomfortable playing a tambourine to two month-old babies that I never went back again. I was not destined for the Boden life.

What to do? Well, initially, I went back to my City job in investment banking when the twins were three months old, and very quickly realised it was never going to work. They were in bed when I left home and in bed when I got back, so I started looking for jobs near my house. The only things going were office-assistant jobs for a third of my wage, but it felt like the right thing to do, so I started all over again as an assistant to the CEO at a housing association.

I got lucky with my boss. She was an incredible, inspirational woman called Geeta Nanda, and she showed me that you can be brilliant at what you do and well respected without being ruthless and walking all over people.

She also told me I was wasted as a PA and made me start to think more of myself. I enjoyed my time there, but soon got a bit bored – and that's when the seed for the wedding-planning business was sown. However, it became clear very quickly that working full time in an office while establishing a new business was not going to work in the long term, and I started looking around for assistant-type roles with more flexible working arrangements.

I found a job just twenty minutes from where I lived and was asked to start immediately. It ticked all the boxes:

Ability to work from home most of the time ☑
Nice variety of work
   (even planning some swanky events) ☑
Great relationship with new boss ☑

I quickly realised that by focusing on the things that were really important to my boss, getting them done extremely quickly and efficiently and being available occasionally at midnight to take a call and rebook him on a flight back from Geneva with no fuss, I was able – just about – to work the hours that suited me without any issues.

We were all happy. I was working to pay off my huge debt (about £30k by this point), my new business was starting to bring in a bit of money and I got to see my kids a bit more.

What I should have known is that just when your ship seems to be sailing smoothly, life has a habit of whipping up a storm in your path. Out of the blue, my boss announced that he was leaving.

'But don't worry,' he told me. 'I know the guy who's coming in. He's a bit young and a bit full-on, but he knows his stuff. You'll be fine.'

If ever there was a case of 'famous last words', this was it.

Day 1. New boss arrived (we'll call him Julien), entering like a pumped-up bull, ready to wreak havoc in our china shop.

I'd already heard that he had his own PA and that he was very keen on bringing her here to work for him. And surprise surprise, very quickly he started dropping hints that my work wasn't good enough and I was lazy (because I left at 5pm each day to get back to the twins). You know, only doing my actual working hours that I was paid for.

He made sure I knew that his previous PA didn't have any kids and was in the office at all hours. I pointed out that these days, we have these things called mobile phones and he could reach me just as easily at home from the golf course as he could at the office, but he had a very clear agenda, and I clearly did not feature in it. Patronising, sexist, arrogant and rude, he represented a generational attitude that still seems to hang around in certain sectors like an unwelcome party guest who steals all your canapés, while moaning that your champagne isn't up to standard.

I tried to stay – I really did. I needed the money. But as the customer in the café where I used to work as a teenager found out when he commented on my boobs and ended up wearing his breakfast, I won't put up with bullying for long.

I walked out, and I was dignified. No money was worth feeling so belittled every day. I knew I'd find a way to move on from this blip. And I did.

Some years later, things were somewhat different for me, and I felt the time was right to serve a dish that, as we all know, is best served cold.

I sent Julien a letter. A letter that I placed casually inside a copy of a recent *Forbes* article featuring a picture of me and how I'd gone from being £30k in debt to a millionaire within a couple of years (it had gone viral).

Here is that letter:

Dear Julien

Some time ago I was working as a PA quite happily (if a bit bored) when my nice boss left and you got hired.

My first clue that you may not be a nice person was when, as you walked in, you pointed at me and shouted, 'Are you the PA? Get me a coffee,' instead of hello, but at that point I had no idea.

That first day you asked me to print out a list of names and photos of the people in our department. These were my friends and colleagues. Lovely people who had worked really hard the last few years. People with families and mortgages to pay.

You then spent half an hour putting big Xs through the faces as you told me these were the people you were going to get rid of so you could bring in your friends from your old company to replace them.

I was horrified that nobody was given a chance and spoke to a colleague.

'He gets the big bucks! That's just how it works when you're a boss,' I was told.

Over the next few weeks, I watched my colleagues disappear one by one while you spent most of your time out of the office during the working day while telling me to cover for you.

When you asked me to do something, I asked for more information so I could see the bigger picture and contribute more. I told you this and you laughed because what could I really offer? I was just a PA. You may as well have patted me on the head.

You don't know this bit but a few weeks in I was looking in your emails as part of my job when I saw a message from you to your old PA telling her you were finding it more difficult to get rid of me because I was actually really good at my job but that you would find a way to do it. Why would you write that knowing I look at your emails?

As a contract PA, there was no HR for me to complain to, but I complained to a couple of directors anyway.

'He's at the top of the food chain. His job is really stressful but he earns the big money so there really isn't much we can do,' I got told again. You were really protected, weren't you?

And you told me how stressful your job was. Constantly. How I couldn't possibly ever understand what it was like. You had temper tantrums often like a toddler storming out of the office. I put up with it, as did everyone else in your boys' club.

You started to try to find fault with my work and I started dreading going to work. Because you were there. In the end I couldn't deal with what an awful, sexist, patronising idiot you were and decided to quit. I handed everything over to your old PA (who was just as awful to me as you – like attracts like).

But I'm actually writing this to thank you, Julien!

Because if it wasn't for you and the patriarchal crap in large corporations everywhere, I wouldn't have been pushed to get out and create the amazing life I have now working for myself, travelling the world, seeing my kids and impacting others.

You made me realise I was never working for someone like you again and the only way to ensure that happened was to start my own business.

If it wasn't for you, I would still be thinking that a leader is someone like you!

Forbes wouldn't have written an article about me that went viral with a quarter of a million views in the first week.

I wouldn't have been able to stand on huge stages helping other women get out from under their bullying bosses and start their businesses.

You being a complete arsehole did all this for me. And them.

I hope life's not too stressful over there still and that your old PA is still enjoying her position.

Lisa x

PS you know those big bucks you were always going on about that caused you so much stress? I earn four times as much as you now 😉

I have no idea if Julien ever read this letter, but after I'd sent it and had a chance to reflect, I had a bit of an epiphany – one that made me more than a bit emotional. (Which for me is an unusual thing, as I tend to only well up at 1980s teen-romance movies.)

I realised that as I'd moved on, taking small steps, the driving force behind my success was the engaged, loyal and passionately committed audience I had cultivated. They were what mattered. They had my back. And they understand what Julien never will: if you stand for injustice, I will not sit at your table.

Growing an Engaged Online Audience

Let's talk about how to grow an audience as loyal and lovely as mine. Because, let's face it, without an audience, you're speaking to an empty room.

Growing a *loyal* audience is so much more important than numbers alone, and we should never get caught up in the notoriously unreliable world of vanity metrics – ways of measuring that make you look good to others but do not actually help you to sell more products. For example, having lots of likes on an Instagram post or 450,000 people 'liking' that TikTok of you lip syncing to Lizzo does not mean they're going to buy anything from you. Ignore the vanity metrics.

Just having a big audience isn't enough.

I have worked with people who have tens of thousands of people in their audiences, but there is no engagement, no atmosphere, no feeling of community. Often, in fact, the lack of connection increases as the audience becomes larger.

Maintaining a level of involvement and engagement as your audience grows is always challenging, but it is crucial to your ongoing success. Which is why you need a *loyal* audience, rather than just an audience.

CULTIVATING YOUR LOYAL AUDIENCE

Fortunately, there are some really simple and easy to follow steps to ensure your audience is a loyal one.

First and foremost, you need to be consistent. You can't write one epic post and then sit back and bask in the glory. This stuff takes time, and today's Dua Lipa can very quickly become tomorrow's Charles & Eddie. (Who? My point exactly!) But don't worry, consistency does not mean constantly, and you do not have to be on social media all day every day to grow an audience. You can have a life, I promise. Here's how:

Take your followers on a journey with you

This is my first point for a reason. It is the basis for everything that will follow. Your audience can't be running along behind you – they need to feel like they are riding shotgun. And this means you must be honest: you should share your ups and your downs. Because honesty and vulnerability will always resonate with your audience way more than any pretence that life is perfect.

I remember when I was starting out, seeing the ranks of perfectly manicured and made-up size-6 business coaches, nibbling quinoa on perfect sandy beaches. At first, it made me feel that I had to fit into this tiny box if I wanted to succeed in the same industry as them. I felt like an outsider. Who would listen to me? I'm not the skinniest or the prettiest or the cleverest or the savviest.

But the more I thought about it, the more I realised that this was the point of me. I was just me. And this social-media-fuelled perception of what and who was acceptable simply didn't matter. The more I thought about it, the more it grated. Because:

a) Size 6 was never going to happen to this size-16 body.
b) Quinoa was never going to happen because Mars bars exist.
c) Me doing what I was told was never going to happen.

And I realised that there must be thousands, if not millions, of women like me: women who had big plans; women who wanted to make a difference; women who didn't want to conform to the norms that were being created; *women who would rather eat fish and chips with gravy than quinoa salad.*

I'd always been an honest person and I knew this had to be the way I went about developing my business and my brand. I needed to be me. This would be my USP. I shared *everything*. The good, the bad and the ugly.

I revelled in my imperfections. I showed my phone propped up on a flowerpot when I did a live to thousands of people. I posted a pic of me in the same, elegant pose as an influencer, lounging on the edge of a crystal-clear pool in Kos. I then posted a video of me scrabbling up the side of the pool to achieve this pose, looking about as graceful as Bambi on ice!

Being imperfect was my superpower. I could be Lisa the business strategist and Lisa the normal girl who shops in Primark.

Your audience needs to hear from you regularly. That's why one of the best ways to nurture an audience and have them get to know what you do is to send regular emails. The problem is that most emails are so impersonal and so intent on 'giving value' that the reader has no idea if they like the person sending them.

Of course, you should give value in emails – you should teach your lovely readers and give them worthwhile content that they can use. This shows your expertise and lets them know they are in good hands. But the reality is that they will be reading emails from other business owners who offer the exact same solution and service or product as you do. So how will they choose who to buy from when they need that service?

They'll buy from the person they like, the person they relate to and the person they remember.

People remember stories. Your stories are how your potential clients will get to know you. It's also how they'll know if they like you.

People regularly tell me that my emails are the only ones they open every week. Our open rate for a fairly big list is super high. I send a weekly email called 'The Friday One' that's pretty popular and has the highest open rate, but because people get used to opening that email, they're also more likely to open one when I'm selling something. And because they've got to know me from

'The Friday One', they're also more likely to buy from me.

Selling is all about building relationships with people and emails can do this so well. Yet so many business owners don't write regularly because they don't know what to write or they believe there has to be huge value in everything they send. And that's just not the case.

Look at secondary messaging

It dawned on me fairly early on that people were not necessarily loyal to me and buying my stuff because they thought I was the best at what I do. They were following me because they liked the other stuff I talked about on social media besides business.

They liked the work I was doing as an anti-bullying campaigner or that I was calling out a lot of the bullshit in the online space. I looked around at others who were doing well and saw that they were talking about other things in their lives, too. Things that mattered to them, things they stood for – anything from fertility and body positivity to work with domestic abuse or sustainability.

As I said earlier: people buy from people they like. But they can't know that they like you and what you stand for if you don't talk about it. I call this secondary messaging. Because yes, you need to talk about what you're an expert in, but to grow a loyal audience you also need to talk about the other stuff that makes you a real person with opinions.

Be consistent

Did I mention consistency earlier? I do believe I did. (In which case, at least I'm consistent!)

To be among the relatively small percentage of people who actually succeed in business, you have to do what the rest won't do – and that, without a doubt, is to keep going when it all seems like a bit of a waste of time.

At the beginning, you will be talking to no one (everyone starts with no one). But give it time. Keep doing it. There are very clear steps in this audience-building journey, and your consistency will see you taking these steps one after the other. It might take you a year or more to build an audience to sell to, but it will be worth it. (Enter the snowball effect – see the following box.) You just need to put the work in now to build a long-term, sustainable passive business model.

THE SNOWBALL EFFECT

- **Stage 1** You will be talking and posting to no one on social media. Just yourself. Maybe your mum. And a few friends might show up to support you. There will be no comments. Just you trying to create a conversation. (Much like trying to talk to a ten-year-old when they are playing Nintendo . . .)
- **Stage 2** Then you'll see it. A comment! One comment from a friend, or maybe a 'nearly friend' from your industry. This is monumental. (But be warned

– there may not be more than a solitary comment for a while.)

- **Stage 3** The next step is a response to this comment from a non-friend. And it is now that what I call the snowball effect kicks in. Suddenly, you have a very engaged and chatty audience who comment on everything you do.

But this does not happen overnight. You have to keep at it. You have to be consistent and you have to keep believing. Because it *will* happen.

When you are new, and your audience is small, you can really use this as a positive thing. Let's say you open a Facebook group or an Instagram account but only a few people join you; make sure your audience look at this as a perk!

Tell those first few that they are 'starting this journey with you' right from the outset, so they'll get unprecedented access to you before there are thousands of followers. They are the ones who will be your biggest ever cheerleaders, so let them know this and make them feel special.

My friend Beth is a hugely successful life and business coach, but she was not a big Facebook fan. Of course, not everyone is, but I could see a large chunk of her ideal clients would be hanging out there and it would be a wasted opportunity not to make the most of this resource.

She created a Facebook group and set about bringing her personality and experience to this new platform. At first nothing much happened. Tumbleweed was blowing through all her social media posts. There just didn't seem to be any traction. It got to the point where she was close to stopping the group, but I urged her to keep going just a little while longer, convinced that the snowball effect would soon kick in.

Sure enough, in month five, everything changed. The comments led to more comments and the engagement went through the roof. She made £45k from that one group that month.

The reality is that your business will probably never be an overnight success. But you never know what's just around that corner – so don't give up.

Be vulnerable and honest

After consistency, these are the two most important things you'll need. Honesty and vulnerability will strike so many chords with so many people it will be worth way more than a perfectly curated Insta feed.

On social media, all we usually see are the best moments, the glitz and the glamour. As I said earlier: comparisons are always unfair because we are comparing the worst we know about ourselves with the best we presume about others. But openness and truly visible vulnerability 100 per cent grows your audience and it also means your life is just that. *Your* life. So: can't be bothered to do your hair? Do a live. Bit cheesed off with the kids' school? Write a quick post about it.

Creating and posting vulnerable content takes courage, especially on social media, but the rewards will be apparent in the way your audience relate to and engage with you.

When you've posted something vulnerable, there may be a lack of response because sometimes people aren't used to this kind of honesty and may not know quite what to say. But whatever feedback or responses you do get, always make sure you engage with everyone. Thank everyone who comments. Seek their input.

This is a major step in building that audience who'll see you as a real person and not just someone who wants to sell to them.

It's not size – it's engagement

There's no denying it's a numbers game. Of course, you'd prefer to have a big audience because then the chances are more people will buy. But a small audience can be just as mighty.

Take my friend and client Abigail Horne, for example, founder of Authors & Co (a publishing company). Abigail had a massive desire to grow her impact, but no wish to have a Facebook group or anywhere that she felt would be 'another thing to manage and show up in' when her passion has always been serving her clients.

Abigail did try a Facebook group for two weeks during the build-up to her latest offering. One hundred and eighty people joined her group to have closer proximity to her, and after those two weeks, she sold £52,000 worth of services (quickly followed by another £74,000 just weeks later).

These figures seem unusually high given the low numbers, but Abigail's community were, and still are, totally engaged with her. To the point where she would say they actually care about each other. So instead of putting time into numbers, Abigail puts her time into two different areas:

- **People** By really getting to know 'her people', Abigail has created loyalty.
- **Her expertise** She delivers a quality and reputable service that others can trust.

Abigail closed the small Facebook group quite quickly (she commits to only putting her focus where she feels she's adding true value), but even without that community, her business continues to generate half a million pounds each year from word of mouth – the mouths of a small, but loyal and engaged audience.

This is a perfect, real-life example of a loyal, smaller audience generating more success than a huge, disinterested and unmotivated one.

The Benefits of a Loyal Audience

You've worked hard to build this following. You've taken them on your bumpy ride, and they seem to have enjoyed the journey. (Well, they're still here with you anyway!) But let's not forget this is a two-way street. They are benefiting from the sense of community, too – the feeling of belonging, the common ground they all share, the safe space where they can vent. (I remember discovering other multiple-birth mums in a dedicated Facebook group, so I can 100 per cent relate.)

Let's take a look at the benefits that this loyal audience brings and the power they possess as a group.

I'm going to start off with some specific examples that come from my personal experience. I always loved to hear first-hand stories like these from people who were further along in their journey than I was, as I felt they brought something tangible and real.

NEVER UNDERESTIMATE THE POWER OF COMMUNITY

As my reputation and my following have grown, so has the number of people who, for one reason or another, want to have a go at bringing me down. I talked about this earlier (see p. 64), but this time it gets a mention purely as the lead-in to something far more positive.

Recently, I was targeted for some pretty full-on abuse. I won't go into specific details for legal reasons, but suffice to say I was called a fraud, a scam artist and a bully, among other things.

Part of me wanted to react, to trade blows, to call out their lies. But I reminded myself of the African proverb, 'The lion does not turn around when the small dog barks', and instead, I replied just once, calmly and succinctly, offering the individual concerned the chance to rethink what she had said, to remove her false allegations and to move on.

My offer was met with derision and further allegations, so that despite the fact that there was no truth behind them they gained more publicity and traction. What now? How to deal with this without fanning the flames?

Well, what happened next was entirely down to my audience and their loyalty to me. They started chatting among themselves about what they could do and within the space of a couple of hours, over 200 of them had reported the offensive post to Facebook. Now, we all know how rare it is to get Facebook, Instagram or any other social media site to take notice of this kind of thing, but they actually went and took the post down!

Would my audience have gone to this much effort if they didn't feel that the community they were a part of – and me, by association – was worth defending? Loyalty goes so much further than people buying stuff.

ORGANIC REACH

I have launched my signature product One To Many® several times, returning a revenue of millions. And I have been able to do this largely without advertising. (I didn't use Facebook ads in any meaningful way until I had made over £1m.) This is because when I post about a course, my lovely, loyal and helpful audience comment on the post telling everyone how good their results have been, and we know there's no better endorsement than that.

GAINING OPPORTUNITIES

One of the first stages I ever spoke on (not counting my youthful forays into amateur dramatics – I once played King Richard, which I only realise now was slightly odd) was one that I shared with Denise Duffield Thomas and Ash Ambirge. You may not all know these names, but I'm guessing a fair few of you will. They are what can be accurately described as big cheeses in the online coaching world who I had looked up to since starting out in the online space. Check them out.

At the time, it is fair to say that I was not a big cheese. (I was a Dairylea cheese triangle, maybe a Babybel at best.) I was definitely not in a place where I should be sharing a stage with people experiencing their level of success. So how did it come about?

Yep, you've guessed it, my audience played their part. Because they had my back and they believed in me, they shouted about me in every space where there was a platform. When events were advertised, they wrote to the organisers and told them they had to get me on their stages. They commented in every chat group. They even got in touch with these mega-successful people themselves, DMing them and telling them they'd be fools not to get me involved in their next event. And whether they really wanted me on their stage or they were just tired of being badgered by loads of women is kind of missing the point. Because either way, it was my audience who played the major part in getting me on that stage, which has led to countless other similar events since.

A Last Word on Your Audience

One of the big things to remember when growing an audience is not to rely solely on social media. At any point, any of the platforms could just decide to shut you down without warning. The way to protect yourself from this is to start growing an email list as well. People will give you their emails, then you can nurture and keep in contact with this audience by emailing them every week (more about how to do this in Chapter 7).

People worry that they will run out of things to say if they email weekly, but you won't. There are so many things to talk about. Your audience just want to hear about you. If you get stuck, then check out the exercise below – I learned it from my copywriter friend Laura Belgray and it works every time.

Exercise: Getting consistent with your message

- Brainstorm what your secondary messaging might be.
- What does consistency mean to you? How many times a week could you commit to posting on social media?
- Research and sign up to a few different mailing lists, so you can start to think of the kinds of weekly emails *you* like to receive.
- Draw a big cross on a page:
  o In section 1 – write three things you've seen in the last twenty-four hours.
  o In section 2 – write three things you heard in the last twenty-four hours.
  o In section 3 – write three things you did in the last twenty-four hours.
  o In section 4 – write three things you've thought in the last twenty-four hours.

This will give you lots of ideas for content to use in emails and on social media to help you grow your audience.

Becoming Visible

A few years ago, I was in Florence and had a bit of a strange experience (besides my *Forbes* interview going viral), and it has stayed with me ever since.

I was there as a student, learning how to write better copy with the fabulous Laura Belgray. (Has it worked? I guess if you're still with me in Chapter 6, then it must have helped!) After we'd finished studying diligently, my husband, Sam, and I decided to make the most of our weekend without the twins and go out for dinner.

We strolled over the River Arno with no real destination in mind, just happy to soak up the sun and revel in the fact that we had nowhere to be at any particular time. After ambling for a while, we came across a beautiful piazza. I mean you couldn't have made it more Italian if you'd wrapped it in a green, white and red flag and drizzled it in olive oil.

Church bells were ringing in the distance, it was still boiling hot at 7pm and I was drinking the most amazing white wine, while people-watching. All in all, I was feeling pretty cosmopolitan. And I was just thinking that all I needed was one of those floppy hats – like Audrey Hepburn wore in those old films where devilishly charming, but slightly roguish leading men smoked cigarettes and drove cool little sports cars – when our perfect picture-postcard piazza dinner was suddenly ruined . . . by Britney Spears.

Around a hundred people of various ages, all wearing questionably bright T-shirts, started dancing on the steps leading up to the cathedral. Now I love a bit of 'Baby One More Time' as much as the next person (in fact, I'm quite renowned for it), but in Florence?

Turns out it was a flash mob and boy, were they into their art! Their moves were something else. We're not talking a little shimmy or two here. We are talking full-on, dramatic, diva-ass-wiggling, splits-while-jumping-off-cathedral-steps-type moves.

But what I really noticed was people's reactions. The people who had just ordered next to us immediately got up, muttering their annoyance about the noise and strutting away to another restaurant. Others looked a bit perplexed about what the hell was happening and returned to their penne puttanesca. But some got up and joined in, dancing away, copying the moves, not giving a damn who was watching them or what they looked like. And the flash mob grew, bolstered by the new spontaneously involved members.

The flash mob were unavoidably visible. They had created something and set it out very boldly in a location that would have maximum effect. Did they care if they were upsetting anyone with their noise? Hell, no; they were too busy enjoying themselves.

This reminded me that we can't be all things to everyone because then we'd all just be boring and vanilla. Not everyone will like us or the things we do in business. And by being controversial or consistently visible, we might annoy some people, but the people who love who we are and what we do will love us even more and realise we're the right one for them because of what we put out there.

Your presence, in whatever medium you choose, is an integral part of you being successful as an online business owner. You can't be that people pleaser, worrying if you've offended someone with the latest post you wrote on Instagram or that email where you said what you really felt (the ones where you close your eyes when you press 'Send'!). Because the people you want to resonate with will love what you do; and the more they see you do it, the more they will think of you when they are deciding who to invest with.

So go for it. Be the flash mob. Stop caring what others think.

Visibility

Initially, I had no intention of writing a whole section focused on visibility, but the more I wrote, the more I realised it was fundamental.

As your audience grows, so will your business, and you'll be clear on the services or products you provide. But the bottom line is you need to be visible. You cannot succeed online unless you realise, accept and embrace the idea that visibility and getting new people to see what you do is 80 per cent of your life in the online space. You may have the best offer, the best service, the best product, but remember this:

Nobody can know, like or trust you if they don't know you exist.

Think of being visible as the simplest form of advertising and marketing. You would expect the businesses and entrepreneurs with the most ability and knowledge or best-quality service or product to be the ones that grab the most customers. But in reality, it is *your* visibility that will draw in your clients – and way before they get to know if you are really any good or not.

You've seen influencers who make a lot of money doing apparently not much, so you know visibility is the key to all this. A potential client needs to see you. Not just once, but many times. They have to get to know you, decide they like what you're about and that you know your stuff – and then buy from you. And don't rely on a Google search to help you out. My first membership was called the GSD society (standing for Get Sh*t Done). But little did I know it was also the acronym for German Shepherd Dogs. Who knows how many sign-ups I missed out on from people who gave up searching for me!

I have a background in acting (no Oscar nominations, but some interesting minor roles) and even I was a bit scared of putting myself out there. But you can be any personality type and still be visible. Plenty of my clients are introverts, but once they start working on their visibility strategy, they can sculpt it and shape it to work for them and lead with their individual strengths.

A MULTI-LAYERED STRATEGY

Once I'd grasped just how important getting seen would be, I got visible very quickly using what I call a multi-layered visibility strategy.

You've probably worked out by now that everything I do is strategic. When you plan things, they usually work and if they don't, then you have learned something and have the metrics there to work with. Visibility is no different, and a social media strategy here is just one part of the game.

The entrepreneurs I looked up to were not just relying on social media or even social media and one other way of becoming visible. They were using social media and then choosing three to five other ways (I call these visibility layers). This makes so much sense because if one thing goes wrong (say, Facebook goes down when you are launching, for example) it won't ruin your business. You'll still have the other layers. It needs to seem that you are everywhere. Of course, you won't be, but it will look that way because you're in different places, often with the same content. And you need to choose the layers that fit well with your ideal client.

We'll start with social media and then talk about some of the other layers.

Social media

Sometimes I'm envious of people who move away from social media and just live the old-fashioned way. But, for an online business, I'm afraid it is crucial.

Remember when you identified your ideal client in Chapter 4? Well, one of the things you have worked out about them is what social media platforms they scroll.

Do not try to be everywhere; just go to where your ideal client hangs out.

My first piece of advice is to choose two platforms, hit them hard and do them well. Don't be afraid to repurpose content. For example, if you have written a blog, you can take short one-liners from it and use them on your Instagram feed. Or if you go live, transcribe your words and use them as a Facebook post. (This reminds me of when my mum would make a roast on Sunday and then, for the rest of the week, we'd be having pies, soups and anything else she could use the leftovers in to keep us going.)

There are loads of advantages to this, the main ones being:

a) **You'll save time and money** – why add more tasks to your day when the content is all there.

b) **When writer's block strikes** – you'll have some popular and applicable content to use.

c) **You'll reinforce your message** – there is an old marketing rule that says your customer needs to hear your message twenty-seven times before they buy (I'm not sure if this is 100 per cent true – after all, 87.6 per cent of all stats are made up on the spot – but I'm sure there is an element of truth in it).

Make sure that what you post links into what you're doing at that time. For example, if you're launching something, make sure the topics you cover are related to the bigger picture.

And schedule for the whole month – have a plan. Maybe even weekly themes that you can share among all your socials.

When Clubhouse was held up as the future of all online businesses, I went on it for five minutes. It was full of bro marketers (see p. 17) peacocking to each other about how amazing they were. It made me feel dirty, so I came straight back off. But I was told immediately that if I did not use the new shiny platform, my business was doomed to fail within six months. Well, that was two years ago and I'm still here. Maybe the same people are still peacocking over there on Clubhouse but everyone else has got bored and left.

Panic is often created around these new platforms, urging you to get in quick before everyone does and they become overloaded. They call it being an early adopter. Usually this is just a vanity metric. (Remember them? See p. 105.) But don't stress it. Stick with wherever your ideal clients are. And if you really want to make sure you're right, you can always ask them. Do a little survey. It's all good for engagement.

The main platforms that most of you will at least have heard of are:

- **Facebook groups and pages** A Facebook page is like a shop window. You can see what they've got, and get a rough idea of the kind of things they sell. But it's impersonal. A Facebook group is a step up from this. It is a safe space where more detailed interactions can take place and advice and support can be shared. When thinking of what to post and where, anything that shows what you do or how you do it can go on a page, but if you want a conversation with your clients, a group is a great place to do it. (Oh, by the way, every six months or so, someone will shout, 'Facebook is dead! Nobody uses it any more except old people.' Ignore them. It's been shouted for the last five years and I'm still making multiple millions every year by being visible mainly on this one platform.)

- **TikTok** This is the new kid on the block (although that depends when you read this), and I think it's probably here to stay. Your kids will be on it. It uses video, which is definitely where most things are going. Do not feel you have to be funny or dance on it – there are accounts making money on TikTok just by being informative – and it's a good one for repurposing stuff you've already posted on Instagram reels.

- **Twitter** One of the first. Seems to be mainly frequented by journalists and Members of Parliament but still useful. It has a fairly small word limit, but I repost to this platform. If I was to get rid of one, this would be the first to go.

- **LinkedIn** Used to be the playground of corporates who would stick a CV on there and hope to be head-hunted but the entrepreneurs have crept over there, too, and can do pretty well on it. Stick some good articles on there and opinion pieces to grow your following and eventually sell.

- **Instagram** This is my second-most used platform. I particularly like the stories function as every day, no matter what I'm doing, I can show quick, behind-the-scenes videos and it's a really great way for my audience to get to know the real me. Plus, stories disappear after twenty-four hours, so if I do something stupid (happens a lot when I've had a drink!), it's not there for too long.

- **Reels are becoming a big thing** – again, video is really important on social. Reels turned me off at first because people I'd admired for years in business suddenly realised they had always wanted to be a comedian/singer/dancer and here was a platform they could do this on while pretending it had something to do with business. Cue thousands of women dancing in their gardens or miming to hip-hop while pointing at random sentences they'd written offering tenuous business advice. It seems to have calmed down somewhat and is being used in a less cringe-worthy way, but don't be surprised if every now and again you have to unfollow someone on there, purely to save yourself from smashing your phone into a million pieces.

- **Ads** You can use ads on Facebook, Instagram, TikTok, etc., but choose wisely. They can work well for getting more audience on your email list, but know the costs – by the time you pay a Facebook ads manager and have a budget for the ads, you can easily be spending thousands per month. My advice is to try to grow organically first (as mentioned previously, I avoided ads until I'd made over a million because I tried early on and lost a fair bit of money, so got scared). Organically has worked well for me, but when I have used ads, I've used an omnipresence strategy. This is where an audience that has liked some of your posts and videos is fed even more of them by Facebook, so that their feed is taken up with you.

Note: don't be surprised if, by the time this book has gone to press and you are reading it, there is a whole host of new platforms!

Other visibility layers

We've looked at social media; now, let's take a look at the other visibility layers you can consider.

- **Talking in other people's memberships** There are so many other entrepreneurs with their online spaces out there. The first hurdle to overcome is to stop seeing them as competitors. Try to change your mindset to one where you genuinely want them to do well. You might even end up collaborating with them in the future. Someone else's achievements have no impact on your own happiness or success. So prepare a great presentation on the topic you feel is your biggest strength, the one that really shows you as an expert, make it so it can be adapted according to the length of time you are given (say, with slides that can be removed or split it into sections), then pitch via email to other groups or memberships with your ideal client and ask the owner of those groups if you can help their audience with a training on your specialist subject. Make sure it's not exactly the same as the owner's expertise, as they will then say no; but if it complements what they do, it will only give value to their audience.

A BRIEF WORD ON SYSTEMS

One of the easiest ways to make yourself stand out and be remembered is to come up with your own system. I mentioned my CASsH® system. This is now uniquely mine and instantly associated with me and my brand. It also gives me a great starting point for any presentation I do. This should always be simply about *how* you do what you do – not what you do. If how you do the thing you are an expert in can be written into a simple, easy-to-understand system with a catchy title, do it!

- **Talking on stages** This is a great way to get that real, face-to-face connection that cannot be replicated. The energy generated from a live event always exceeds that of a virtual one. It stands to reason that you're unlikely to be asked to join Tony Robbins or Oprah on stage at the start of your business journey, but this doesn't mean that this visibility avenue is a dead end.

- **Look for small networking events in your area** Eventbrite is really useful for this. Find groups that you think would be interested in what you have to say. Think about your ideal client and the groups they may attend. Then go along one day and once you have met the organiser, contact them to see if you can talk. Don't be scared, just do it! What's the worst that could happen? They say no? Ok, then you try the next one. Then start to pitch to the bigger stages. Because, remember, no one is going to approach you – you have to get yourself out there. But bear in mind, the larger stages will often only accept speakers with a reasonably substantial audience. That work on growing an engaged audience? Get on it!

THE ROAD TO SUCCESS AT A SPEAKING GIG

Once you have secured your first speaking gig, remember a few basic tips to ensure it goes well:

- **Practise, practise, practise** Rehearse out loud. Take your time. Remember to breathe and to pause, especially just before impactful elements of your talk. This works well to get the audience engaged.

- **Always time your speech** Do this a few times to make sure you don't overrun or come up short.
- **Start with something attention-grabbing** Something personal is good here, or a strong quote. This helps to establish your credibility, connects you to the audience and creates the right emotional atmosphere. Then take a pause and let it sink in (this is also good for your nerves) before moving into the middle and the close.
- **Know the set-up of where you are speaking** Check it out when you visit as a spectator, and then arrive nice and early on the day to make sure everything runs smoothly.
- **Relax** Try to enjoy yourself. This shouldn't be a punishment and nerves are not your enemy. Adrenaline will help you, but remember to pause and breathe.
- **Remember why you are there** You want to get visible, thereby making yourself known to more people who could become your clients. You want them to sign up. Simple as that.

- **PR** There is still no better credibility grabber than an 'as-seen-in' heading on your website or social media. Rightly or wrongly, the general perception of someone who is featured in the media is that they are an expert. (Maybe not if you're sharing your story of how your cat channelled the spirit of Marie Antoinette in a *Take a Break* magazine article, but in most other cases!) Every magazine, TV show and online medium has to fill its pages or its time slots. They will need articles, interviews or just talking-head snapshots (where they want just a quote from an 'expert'). The point is, they will always need content. So don't think that you must have a PR person when you start out. I got some of my biggest articles (like *Forbes*, *Psychologies* magazine and national papers) by myself. Just be prepared to be ignored a lot, or at best get a 'No, thank you' before you hit on something. However, when things do start to pick up in your business, it is a very sensible move to work with a PR expert who can get you noticed by more and more media channels, leaving you to focus on doing what you do best.

- **Becoming an author** One of the best ways to get visible (and show your expertise) is to write a book. You can get a traditional book deal where the publisher pays you an advance to write your book and markets it for you in bookshops; or you can self-publish, where you pay a company to publish your book to be put on Amazon. Many businesses choose to self-publish these days, not least because getting a traditional book deal isn't easy, but also because you have more control over things like the price and the content.

- **Podcasts** Before you start up your own podcast, it is a really good idea to get featured on others as a guest. You'll pick up their audience as a result, but only if your ideal client is there. Early on in my career, I spoke in groups that were hugely spiritual, where my straight-talking, 'you-make-your-own-choices' outlook did not always go down well. So do your research, choose the podcasts you want to be on and pitch. If you do go the podcast route, you'll gain even more visibility if you get to the top of the business charts. I got to number 1 in the UK business charts, which was great, but don't sacrifice your integrity to do it (for example, there are podcast managers who will give you a strategy whereby people review you even before they've listened to get you there – possibly into an obscure category for five minutes). Don't go down this road. It's misleading and, ultimately, it's a vanity metric.

CREATING YOUR OWN PODCAST

Having your own podcast is not difficult, but there are some simple tips to bear in mind:

- **Identify *why* you want to make a podcast** For the purposes of this chapter the answer will be for visibility and audience growth, but there may be other, equally important reasons – sharing your passion, for example.
- **Work out who your podcast is for** Your work on your ideal client will help you with this.
- **Give people a reason to listen** This means talking about stuff that will really resonate with your listener when they tune in.
- **Think ahead** Don't just think about one episode. Try to write down topics of interest for at least ten or fifteen shows before you get recording,
- **Know that having a podcast is a slow burn** You won't get new clients from it immediately. It takes time.
  There is also the techie stuff – getting the right gear,

learning how to edit, obtaining music etc. – but there are loads of useful online guides that can help you with all this.

If you'd like help with your podcast you can find more information here: audio.lisajohnson.com/podcast

How to Pitch (for Everything!)

You have to learn how to pitch yourself to all of the above super-useful and always-available platforms. As I said earlier, no journalist will be sat at their desk thinking, Ooh, maybe if I go online, I can find some really interesting entrepreneurs and ask them really nicely if they'd like to feature in my magazine.

This means growing a thick skin. And it all starts with building relationships. Work out everything and everyone you like online – the people who resonate with you, those you respect or are intrigued by or those who seem to share your values and goals. Or all of these.

Think about podcasts/journalists/influencers/business owners and start to be extra involved in what they do. Like their posts and comment on them, so that they start to see you. This will then lead to you asking if you can be involved in any way. But don't just go in cold; think of an angle that reflects something that's happening in the world, so that it's more likely to be relevant right now. No one cares about a bog-standard press release; the average journalist receives hundreds if not thousands of these every day, and they are immediately filed in 'Trash', so you have to come up with something that will grab their attention:

- **Ensure you have an interesting and eye-catching subject line** You don't want your approach to be ignored because the subject line is boring. (Stats show that 47 per cent of emails are opened based on the subject line alone.) Keep it brief, and don't give too much away.
- **Know who you're pitching to** Do some research and find out the name of the relevant person. ('Dear Features Editor' never goes down well). And actually listen to the podcast or read the magazine in question.
- **Create your pitch for your recipient** Explain why their audience would benefit from you and your knowledge. Also, the audience of each publication you are aiming for will change every time, and so should your pitch to reflect this – they can tell when you're copying and pasting.
- **Make it relevant** During lockdown, thousands of experts realised now was the time to get their knowledge out there. From articles on working from home without killing your kids, to health coaches advising on how to improve your immune system, to personal trainers showing you how to work out in your home . . . This is the kind of approach you will need to take. And while you should never lead with your bio, make sure to add a little bit about yourself at the end. Here are examples of good and bad bios, complete with commentary:

Good

Lisa Johnson is a seven-figure strategist specialising in helping entrepreneurs scale their businesses using passive income from memberships and courses. [**One brief sentence that describes me.**]

After a tough childhood spent in social housing, Lisa

went on to have successful careers in law, banking and the entertainment industry. Her background in overcoming obstacles has helped mould her into a bold, straight-talking coach, who is never afraid to be an authentic and outspoken truth teller.

She has spoken on the BBC's *Woman's Hour* and is a Thrive Global contributor. She has been featured in national newspapers and magazines, including *Psychologies*, the *Guardian* and *Red*. A recent feature on Lisa in *Forbes* magazine garnered over a quarter of a million views in a week. [**Relevant experience in a couple of paragraphs. What have I done that would impress people?**]

Lisa is a huge believer that everyone can become a success, no matter their background, and is known for her anti-bullying campaigning online. [**My philosophy – telling people something that sets me apart.**]

Lisa lives in Bedfordshire, UK with her husband and ten-year-old twin sons, but coaches around the globe. [**One final sentence covering personal details.**]

Bad

Hi!

I'm Lisa and I'm a business strategist. [**And? Where is the detail?**]

I've been through a lot growing up and I think that is what makes me much more relatable. [**What have I been through and why does it make me relatable?**]

After leaving school, I had a number of different jobs, including acting, banking and being a PA. I then gained a degree in law before starting my own wedding-planning business, which led to others asking for my advice and eventually this grew into my coaching business. [**This is just a list – boring.**]

I really enjoy being interviewed in magazines and podcasts and my goal is to give a TED Talk in the future. [**Which magazines? What about? So – I haven't actually done a TED Talk yet?**]

When I'm not coaching, I like to hang out with friends. [**Not much personality here.**]

Make pitching for visibility part of your weekly strategy. And as before, don't forget that this is a numbers game. Keep trying and don't give up. Just remember J. K. Rowling and her twelve rejections!

KATE'S STORY

Kate is the owner of The Full Freezer; she works with individuals, groups, corporations and brands to cut food waste in homes and workplaces across the world. Here, she explains her visibility story in her own words:

The first time I came across Lisa it was in late 2020, through Facebook. I remember thinking that she spoke a lot of sense and that she could help me move my business forwards, but I had massive resistance to the idea of spending £2k with someone I hadn't even heard of a week earlier.

At some point, she mentioned her feature in Forbes, *and of course the first thing I did was look it up. It provided me with all I needed to know; she was legitimate and didn't just talk a good game. I could see from her website that she had been featured in other publications, too, and so my mind was made up.*

Before the course had even started, Lisa had taught me something . . . visibility matters.

The course itself wasn't about visibility, but she touched on her own PR journey during the trainings and her free content, and through her, I ended up signing up to her friend Selena Soo's 'Impacting Millions' PR course. This taught me how to strategise and be purposeful with my PR and visibility.

I must confess that in the early days, I was terrified at the thought of being in the press or on TV, but Lisa and Selena helped me to see that the haters who come from being visible are not important. There will always be bullies and people that don't like what you're doing. What is important is that you are visible to the people who need your help. Staying hidden is not just a disservice to yourself, but a disservice to those who can benefit from your knowledge and expertise. And without stepping out of the darkness, I honestly don't think I would have a business.

By perfecting my messaging and nailing my pitch, within fifteen months, I have landed features on BBC Food, BBC News, in the Telegraph, *the* Sun *and* Prima *Magazine and have even had my story picked up and featured on the* Drew Barrymore Show. *I have also appeared on brilliant podcasts such as Jen Gale's* Sustainable(ish), Let's Do Lunch *with Jenny Tschiesche and Lisa's very own podcast,* Making Money Online.

Selena's expert advice helped to guide me through my first live TV spot on Steph's Packed Lunch *and a live cook-along with Michelin-starred chef Tom Kerridge, as well as slots on breakfast TV and many radio shows, sharing my tips and advice around reducing food waste.*

And, most importantly, this visibility has helped me to secure paid work, often without even having to seek it out! I have been approached by brands such as Birds Eye, Thermapen and Love

Food Hate Waste, and have even had to turn other brands down due to exclusivity agreements and my capacity.

I have gone from feeling stuck and frustrated about how to attract more clients, to having the confidence that there are endless organisations and individuals I can help. My corporate Lunch and Learn sessions have blown up, and I have become 'the person' to come to if you want to reduce your household food waste.

This visibility has helped to reassure the individuals I work with that my work is legitimate, in the same way that Lisa's Forbes article convinced me, and has supercharged my audience growth, which at the time of writing sits at around 40,000 people across Instagram and my Facebook group.

I still can't quite comprehend that so many people now know my name and my face, and I have no desire (nor will I ever have!) to be famous. But it is amazing to think how much food is being saved from landfill because I decided to show up, share my message and get visible!

You can find out more about Kate at thefullfreezer.com

I love this story so much, and did you notice that it was my visibility that got Kate's attention in the first place? If there is anything backs up all that I have taught you in this chapter, it is this.

Fear of Being Visible

Let's face it, the main reason business owners aren't visible isn't because they don't know how to be. It's because they fear it. What if they're judged? What if people think they have no idea what they're talking about? Some people even worry about what they look like. (I swear one of my eyes looks bigger than the other. I'd never noticed it until I did my first Facebook livestream and then that's all I could see.) Or what they sound like: what if they forget their words or say 'um' too many times?

Well, there's only one way to stop these fears. And that's to stop making it about you.

Drop the ego.

Harsh, but true. Because when we think these thoughts, it's all about us: what *we* look like; what people will think about *us*. Instead, make it about them. You know – the people you're being visible for. Those people out there who need your help and need to hear from you. And once you understand that, you won't care so much because you know that one person who desperately needs to hear what you have to say today will not be worrying about what you look like (or that your left eye is bigger than the right!). And if they do? Well, then you don't really care about them, anyway.

Visibility is the biggest part of making money online, so find that confidence and go for it!

Exercise: Become more visible

- Write down ten topics you would feel comfortable talking about for three minutes. These will be your first livestreams.
- Formulate the structure of a presentation on the topic you feel most like an expert on. You don't need to write the entire thing, but just by writing the headings, you'll see that you have a lot to say and could easily fill a presentation.
- Find five memberships you could pitch to train in where the ideal client is similar to yours.
- Identify a publication you'd love to write an article for. Who is the features editor? Where would your article sit in that magazine? This will help you get ready to pitch.

CHAPTER 7
Systems That Will Make Your Life Easier

I'd made it. I was running my own business.

Well, I say I'd made it. Although that would indicate that I knew where I was going and had arrived at my destination, which is about as far removed from the truth as you could imagine.

My business seemed to organically grow. Like it had a mind of its own. When I look back, I see it as Audrey II in *Little Shop of Horrors*, insisting that I continue to feed it. Still, I seemed to be creating a name for myself as a business mentor, and as I kept up the feed of clients, a steady stream of new ones appeared very quickly.

It stands to reason that my first year in business was crazy. I was chock-a-block doing one-to-ones and running my Facebook group. Life was moving at a thousand miles an hour and I was riding the crest of this wave, feeling insanely excited, a little bit scared and just a tad baffled that people would want to pay me to talk to them about running their businesses.

I made six figures in six months, which was three times what I'd made in a year in my previous job, so there was definitely an element of sitting back and rubbing my hands together, thinking, Wow, this is great.

But then along came a defining moment. This was neither a business lightbulb moment, driven by innovation and clarity, nor a chance encounter with an inspirational personality who made me reassess my purpose in life. In fact, it was a moment of forgetfulness, fuelled only by being too busy and spinning too many metaphorical plates.

The twins had started at a new school in the village where we lived, and we wanted to make sure they made a good impression. (As an aside, they have always been quite opinionated and able to articulate their thoughts clearly. This is generally a good thing, but not quite so positive when on their second day Finnian spent quite some time explaining to their new head teacher why Pluto wasn't a planet, and that they needed to replace all the astronomy textbooks in the library immediately.) But all appeared to be going well. They had their uniforms, book bags and all the other paraphernalia and seemed to be settling in ok.

However, what didn't go down very well was when, on the first day of their second week, I forgot to pick them up the first time I was scheduled to do this job. Yes, the very first time! So engrossed in my work, with my phone on silent, that they ended up sitting there alone with their teacher for forty minutes.

You should have seen their faces. Cue 'mum guilt'. There is no other guilt like it, and it lasted ages.

This defining moment resulted in an honest appraisal of my circumstances. Yes, it was great having made six figures very quickly. But what was not so great was working so hard for so many hours that my most important task of the day was forgotten.

Of course the boys got over it, and, other than being thought of as a less-than-shining beacon of parenthood by their teacher for a couple of weeks, no serious damage was done. I still felt crappy, though; and more than a little bit peeved that entrepreneurialism and parenthood were clearly not cut out to be buddies.

But that was not acceptable! How could I change things? I was grateful and proud that I'd created this business that I was good at, and which provided me with a good income, so I'd be mad to stop now, wouldn't I?

Well, yes. And no.

The hours in the day were set in stone, but my creativity was limitless.

I just needed to find a way of working that allowed me to serve more people, not just one at a time.

So I did what I always do. I researched, I learned and I planned.

And then I realised that the one-to-many passive income business model could indeed be life-changing as it would allow me to decide when I wanted to work. But it wasn't going to just create itself while I slept. To run this style of business I needed consistency (there it is again). And to achieve the necessary level of consistency, I was going to need some help. And I don't just mean getting my husband, Sam, to pick the boys up from school.

In the course of my research, I found out that there were numerous ways to use technology to automate what I did. I didn't have to write a new email each day and remember to send it off. There were lots of ways that technology could take over these admin tasks from me.

Here's a neat little summary showing how automation in my business transformed the way I worked:

Year 1:
Revenue – £220k
Hours worked – around seventy per week

Year 2:
Revenue – over £1m
Hours worked – around thirty per month

(Oh – and now I never forget to pick the kids up; mainly because I have a childminder who does it for me, but it's the principle, isn't it?)

What the Heck is Automation?

Techopedia defines automation like this: the creation and application of technologies to produce and deliver goods and services with minimal human intervention.

I, on the other hand, define it like this: anything that means I can earn money while doing the things I love, i.e. being on holiday!

I can't even begin to count the number of times I have heard friends, clients or peers say these five words: 'I'm not a techy person.' And I get it; I've said it, too. Because, let's face it, the majority of us are intimidated by 'the tech stuff'. But social media and the good old Internet have created a space where thousands of little tools have been developed and can be readily accessed so as to make the life of an online business owner much easier. It is so easy to embrace these systems; we just need to get over that techy speed bump – because, ultimately, automated systems are there to make life easier. By finding the right things that work for *you* and *your* business, rather than the hottest new options, you are investing in the longevity of your business and improving your clients' experience, while cutting down on the amount of time spent doing your back-of-house work.

Sales Funnels

The most effective and valuable automated system for your business is called, quite simply, a funnel.

A sales or business funnel (you'll hear it called loads of different names, including a marketing funnel or leads system, but they're all the same thing) shows the route your customers take from first becoming aware of your brand to buying from you. This is my favourite analogy: think of a sales funnel as finding a particular fish's favourite bait, then throwing it out there so only that type of fish is attracted to it.

Of course, you could always hope that people just find your weekly emails or just stumble across your website and look at the exact thing you want them to buy. But truth alert: that is not going to happen. You know that line, 'If you build it, they will come'? Well, that's a lie. You need to build it, go get them and pull them in.

I've known so many people who have paid money and spent a lot of time creating a shiny, all-bells-and-whistles website that no one ever looks at. In fact:

You don't even need a website to run your business.

For the first year or so, a website should not be high on your list of priorities. Sure, it'll look good – but if no one knows it's there, you may as well write your shopping list and put it on there.

A sales funnel removes the 'hit-and-miss' factor. It consists of a series of communications designed to get your ideal client to go where you want them to, see what you want them to see and, ultimately, buy what you want them to buy. These 'communications' could be Facebook ads, blogs, social media posts, emails or something else. But they all start with you putting something out there that will attract your fish – your ideal client; it's a bit like going up to them, tapping them on the shoulder and showing them what they need. No waiting or hoping required. And the great thing is that once you've set it up, it's automated – so it all happens while you're doing other things.

Using our fishing analogy again, your customers might not take the bait at first, but you've brought something to their attention that you are pretty sure they will like, and you've got them interested. Remember, people's lives are busy. Sometimes they don't make decisions immediately, and you won't always get a sale on the first visit to a sales page. But by bringing them into your sales funnel, you have started the process of turning them from bystanders into customers.

Next, you show them a little more by emailing them with more value and posting content on social media, engaging them in topics they find interesting. And they move in closer. Some might have a nibble at the bait, while others will hang back and wait to see what else happens. You will never reel them all in, but there will be plenty who are enticed by what is on your hook.

It's all about educating potential clients in more detail about what you do, what you have to offer and why it could be right for them.

The advantages here are clear. It means your sales strategy is personalised, so the whole experience will be a positive one for your ideal client. Plus, as your series of communications develops, you will weed out those people who just aren't right for you.

There are different stages to a sales funnel, varying according to who you are learning from, but they are generally as follows:

- **Stage 1: Awareness** You can't make a sale if your ideal clients don't know who you are. So the idea here is to create awareness of your brand, getting them to start to relate to your content, and nudging them in the direction of taking action. This will come via you offering some free value. Think about when you may have signed up for something yourself – maybe you've seen a free guide to starting a business on a Facebook post and given your email in exchange for it. That's the bait.

- **Stage 2: Interest** Once people have learned about your brand because they've signed up for your free offer and you've sent them some emails, you'll want them to start taking a more active interest. You could say your fish is now hooked, but still needs reeling in. So your content at this stage has to be around building a relationship with your potential client, keeping the conversation going, giving them more value and getting them to know you even better as a personal brand.

- **Stage 3: Decision** At this stage of the funnel, people are taking a very keen interest in your product or service. They are ready to buy, but they need to trust that you're the right person. So this is the time to make your offer irresistible and talk about why you *are* the right person to buy from.
- **Stage 4: Action** Now they have made their decision, the client acts and purchases your product or service and becomes part of your business's ecosystem. That doesn't mean your work here is done, though. You want this to be the first of many purchases, so you need to make sure you focus on customer retention by continuing to communicate with your client by email.

Choosing the Right Tech

All your communications so far can be set up so that they are sent automatically. There are so many automated systems that can do this for you and more appear on the market all the time. Some are free and some are paid for but have more bells and whistles. The popular systems at the time of writing are Kartra, MailerLite and Kajabi, but it's worth doing a little research to see what will work best for you. They all are super easy to use – they basically do it all for you (other than write your content).

WHAT IS A CRM SYSTEM?

CRM stands for Customer Relationship Management, and it basically does what it says on the tin: it's software for managing your relationships with customers. The three systems I mentioned above all incorporate CRM systems.

When you break it down, most CRM systems keep lists of email addresses you have collected from people signing up to your lead magnet (that thing you used as bait above) and they usually have a function to set up emails to go out to some or all of those people. Some can also write sales pages for people to buy your stuff from, too (we think of these as 'all- in-one' systems).

Any type of system that uses data to develop and improve customer relationships can be known as 'CRM', but it has come to refer mainly to specific software or technology.

A CRM system can also collect and store all the data you have for potential and existing customers across every touchpoint in their journey (a touchpoint is any time a potential or current client comes into contact with you – your business/your brand – before, during or after they purchase something from you). This could be details shared through forms or engagement with your social media or emails. It's useful because it will help you learn more about their needs and what they like.

From the moment you go online with your business, there is really useful information to be had about your clients and potential clients, so having a system that helps you make the most of this is a massive help when it comes to increasing your efficiency and turning those 'maybes' into 'definitelys':

A CRM captures your potential clients and moves them automatically into your sales process.

A CRM can also act as a super-efficient virtual office manager.

But there's loads of other stuff that different tech systems can do, meaning you're not stressing where you don't need to, and are able to focus your time on what you really want to do:

- **Scheduling appointments with automated confirmation and reminder emails,** then syncing those appointments with your external calendar, so you don't have to worry about getting double booked.
- **Storing all documents and communications** in one convenient central place where your clients can access them.
- **Setting reminders** about internal tasks that need to get done.

All the good systems are really easy to customise, so you can tweak and play around to set them up how you want them. There are loads out there, and they usually have 'Free for two weeks' deals, plus instructions/manuals online. So they really aren't intimidating, and the long-term benefits are huge.

Why You Need Automation

From systems that show you the data of who has looked at which of your emails right through to others that schedule your social media posts for you, there is a tech tool for everything, and regardless of whether you see yourself as a technophobe or not, they are all worth exploring to see where time can be saved.

There are six main areas where automated tools can really help:

1 **Handling enquiries**: keeping notes of who has contacted you and when and what the outcome was.

2 **Ongoing client management**: keeping a record of any calls, what was said and when.

3 **Finances**: allowing people to pay for your service and keep records on what they paid and when.

4 **Marketing (especially email)**: sending out emails to different people who have signed up to receive them and keeping records of what was sent to whom and when.

5 **Time management**: scheduling your day, booking appointments and keeping track of your time.

6 **Project management**: helping you to work out what needs to be done and when and sending tasks to a team, if you have one.

Take your pick!

TIME BLOCKING

When I started out, I'd always fall back on my old favourite, the 'to-do list', thinking that this was the way to stay on top of the stuff I needed to get done. But with a to-do list, you tend to do the easy and the quick-to-get-done things, so you can cross them off, while the tough tasks, the ones that take time and effort, simply stay on your list when you rewrite it the next day.

So how do you balance all the things that absolutely need doing every day – the strategic and the challenging; the creative and the admin – ensuring that you are focused and bringing your best to the things you really care about?

This is where time blocking comes in. It's simple but so effective, and it's totally changed the way I go about my day.

Time blocking works perfectly in the following scenarios:

- **If you have a lot of different projects or responsibilities** It stands to reason that this will apply to everyone at the start of their online business journey. It'll be just you at the beginning, so your skillset is going to need to be broad by necessity.
- **If you get caught up by 'shiny-object syndrome'** You get distracted by the email that's just landed or the Facebook post that you just have to comment on.
- **If you find it hard to find the time to work *on* your business rather than *in* it** Your strategic approach isn't always what it could be, and you end up being more reactive than proactive.

> Time blocking is a simple but effective time-management method that asks you to divide your day into blocks of time.

Each block of time is dedicated to a specific task, or group of tasks, and only those tasks. This does away with the bad old to-do list (because all tasks are given equal ranking in terms of importance), replacing it with a schedule that clearly states what you'll work on and when.

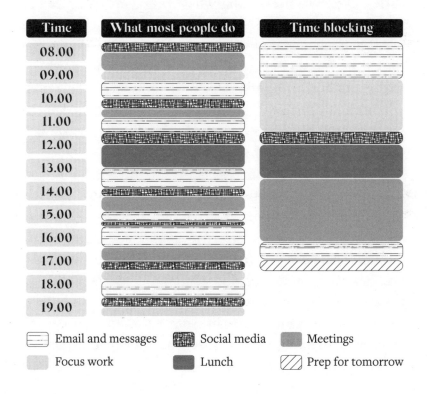

Time	What most people do	Time blocking
08.00		
09.00		
10.00		
11.00		
12.00		
13.00		
14.00		
15.00		
16.00		
17.00		
18.00		
19.00		

▤ Email and messages   ▦ Social media   ▨ Meetings
▨ Focus work   ■ Lunch   ▨ Prep for tomorrow

Plan Ahead

Now of course, those of you who are easily distracted may still be tempted to move your time blocks around or jump to the thing you like best. The key here is prioritising your task list in advance.

For this, you'll need a weekly review, where you can see what you've got happening in the week ahead, and then plot out your time blocks (see box on p. 155) for each day. I allow fifteen to twenty minutes every Sunday evening to get this done.

By time blocking your days in advance you are doing away with any umming and ahhing and leaning towards those easier tasks when deciding what to do. Instead, you just stick to your schedule. And the best thing is you'll never get overwhelmed again – because while you're doing that important piece of client work on a Monday morning, and find yourself starting to stress over the social media posts you haven't done yet, you can relax in the knowledge that you have time blocked them in for Wednesday at 2pm. So you can forget about them until then.

It seems so obvious and so simple, right? Well, it is – but it is remarkably effective, too. And it's not just me who thinks so. Cal Newport, author of *Deep Work: Rules for Focused Success in a Distracted World*, dedicates twenty minutes every evening to scheduling out the next work day. Cal describes how detailed planning generates massive productivity. He reckons a forty-hour time-blocked working week creates the same output as an unstructured sixty-hour working week. As you would expect, there are loads of apps out there to help you do this in the most efficient way – check them out!

I'd like to share a case study of one of my clients who started time blocking and the amazing effect it had on her work.

JULIE'S STORY

Julie Gibson started a unique book subscription box business in 2020 after her previous business closed down during the pandemic. While the new business did grow during the first year, it was when she started taking time blocking seriously that things really took off.

Julie launched and ran the box for the first year using the traditional to-do-list approach, but found herself doing the classic ticking-off-the-quick-and-easy-tasks-to-feel-she-had-made-progress thing. Which meant the day-to-day tasks of running the business and delivering the product were eating up all her time before she ever got to those bigger projects that would make a real difference to the bottom line. All the exciting stuff was left languishing at the bottom of a list, while she was left feeling she didn't have enough time in the day to get everything done.

A year into the business and with subscriber numbers stubbornly stuck at around fifty, Julie decided a different approach was needed and started to properly implement time blocking. She believes one of the most important things about this is getting real with yourself about how much time you have available for work, so she started out by blocking in all her family commitments and 'life chores', along with breaks and recreation time.

Then, after programming in essential operational tasks, she was able to see the time available for business-development projects. But, more importantly, she now felt confident that she could stop operational tasks at the end of a time block and work on business development because she knew she had plenty of time programmed in to finish the essential tasks within deadlines.

This new approach means Julie has now completed several important development projects and her subscriber numbers, as well as her income, have more than quadrupled in the space of six months. With her work mapped out in her calendar, she no longer feels like she should be working seven days a week in order to be successful.

Julie has a brilliant semi-passive income stream now, selling a subscription box membership.

You can find out more about Julie at www.theend-oftheworldreadingclub.com

Prioritise Your Workload

Having an online business means you will feel you have a million and one things to do. Especially at the beginning. Use your time wisely.

When I started, I had a full-time PA job, my fledgling business and small twins. This meant the only time I could work on my business was from 6–7am, my lunch hour and 7–9pm, when the kids were asleep. And this meant I had to be very intentional with my time. I had to ask myself constantly: 'Is what I'm about to do a money-generating activity?' In other words, would what I was spending my time on eventually lead to me being paid. If it was a no, then I didn't do it. I needed money to be my focus, so I could afford to outsource tasks and get my time back.

We all love a good networking session, but the truth is we generally end up speaking to the people we know already, so it's not going to bring us new clients. Prioritise what you do always, and don't be afraid to say, 'No' (and you don't have to think up an excuse to justify it either).

The word 'no' is a whole sentence.

Exercise: Start using systems

- Do a bit of research on the systems that could help to automate your business life: for a week, write down the tasks you do on a daily basis, and consider what you would like taken off your plate. Now spend time researching any automated systems that could do those tasks for you – or at least help with them.
- Try time blocking for one week by filling out time blocks for the week ahead with the things you know you need to do. If the time blocks aren't right for your day, create your own on a spreadsheet.

CHAPTER 8
How to Successfully Launch Your Passive Income Product

Teachers, boyfriends, the odd judge here and there – they all told me I'd never amount to much. And when you are young, you tend to start believing the things you are told on a regular basis, especially if the people saying them are the fonts of all knowledge and truth, more commonly known as 'grown-ups'.

But as I grew and learned, I developed a personality trait that has stood me in good stead to build a business that runs in the way I want it to. It should also be said that it has led me to distance myself from some people and seen me enter the odd heated debate with others.

The trait in question is two-pronged:

Firstly, if you tell me something, I'll need to see proof. And I'll want to see this proof verified by several sources – not just because John from the pub told you or all your friends on Facebook say it's so.

Secondly, if you tell me I can't do something, I reckon you'll have at least doubled the chance that I will do that very thing! One of the main reasons why I'm now a multi-millionaire is because someone in my first year of business told me I'd never be anything. (I'll tell you all about that in Chapter 9.)

All of this is basically a roundabout way to lead in to a story about my law degree, which I undertook in response to one such assessment of my prospects. I was at a stage in my life that was very much sink or swim, and thought that if I could prove to myself that I had the skills for something as tough as a law degree in my late twenties then, well, surely anything else would be a walk in the park. Or a paddle in the shallows, at least.

I signed up, not really knowing what this endeavour would entail, but knowing I'd give it my best shot. I was working full-time in an office, but the university sent me all the books I needed in the September and I studied in my tiny studio flat every evening after work and took the exams in the May. I did this for four years.

I learned a lot of interesting things (plus a whole load of not-so-interesting things) and I met an assortment of colourful and intriguing characters every year when travelling to Newcastle to take the exams. One of the most memorable was a guy we shall call Donald.

Donald was old school. I mean this in an appropriately double-entendre way, in that he acted in an extremely old-school manner, but he was also educated at a very old school. Unsurprisingly, then, his attitude towards me was a patronising mix of thinly veiled contempt coupled with a hefty dollop of pretty blatant sexism. I was, in his mind, the archetypal working-class, council-house female. A tick in the diversity box.

Donald was very happy to let me know that he was going to graduate with a first. That he had finished top of his class at school. That the legal profession was in his blood. And that, in fact, he was a bona-fide genius and no one else in our class would get anywhere near him.

Now, I'd love to say that Donald was a fantasist, that he was not extremely intelligent and his comeuppance was just around the corner, but it pains me to say he was very clever indeed. But when he condescendingly muttered that I would be lucky to even finish the degree, let alone pass, he made a serious mistake.

Yes, Donald was naturally clever and had the right accent and wore the right tie, but I had other strengths. (There were times when, looking back, I wished they were strengths like Eleven's in *Stranger Things* but alas, those were not at my disposal.) Years of being picked on and judged and underestimated had led to me cultivating diligence and dedication, plus an ability to strategically plan, prepare and absorb information. These would be my superpowers.

For months, I used these assets to the full. I crammed and I read, I studied and I learned. My social life was non-existent, but I knew that when judgment day arrived, I would be in the best possible position to achieve my potential.

The end result? Did I rub Donald's nose in the fact that I got a first and he didn't? Well, no, actually, because that's not what happened, and that isn't the point of this little story.

I'm not even sure what Donald got, but I passed with a very high 2:1 and, despite stressing a little at the time over what I could've done differently to turn that into a first, I was dead chuffed. No – I was more than that . . . I was absolutely beside myself with satisfaction, happiness and pride. I'd never even done A levels, and had arrived at this incredible moment not by luck, nor by having a brain that just kind of 'got this stuff'. I had reached it by being prepared. By understanding that to get the result I wanted I had to focus, and I had to plan. I needed what I would now call, with my business head on, a strategy.

We all know those classic clichéd, 'inspirational' quotes. The ones that are always plastered over meeting-room walls in every office around the country. But there's one that really does make sense:

Fail to prepare, prepare to fail.

Which brings me to the point of this chapter: I am going to be talking about how to launch your product – and the way to give yourself the best possible chance of a successful launch is to put in the legwork and make sure you are *totally prepared*.

None of us has a guaranteed right to succeed. But there are, as usual, steps you can take that will put you firmly in the best possible position for success.

Prepare for Success

Now that you've read the story preceding this section (I hope you have – I put a lot of work into these stories, you know!), you'll be very aware that preparation is key.

By now, you will also have decided what your product is going to be. Your course, your membership, your ebook or whatever should be the best platform to turn your knowledge into a viable product that your ideal client will want to snap up. **Note:** you don't need to have actually written it at this stage. I know it feels risky but trust me here. You don't want to spend hours creating something, then put it out there only to find that nobody wants it. What you learn throughout your launch process will help you to shape the perfect product designed specifically for your ideal client and their needs, so you can write the course as you go along.

You've also grown your audience and become visible, but – without wishing to sound like a stuck record – don't expect this to take twenty minutes. You cannot rush this. Some things take time to achieve, so you need to be prepared to work step by step. And it doesn't matter how small your steps are.

You can do a lot with small steps.

A little heads-up here, before we go any further. The standard conversion rate is around 1–2 per cent (that's how many of your audience are likely to turn into buyers when you launch), so they say (I don't know who 'they' are, but it's a widely known stat). My clients get conversion rates much higher than this, but let's go with worst-case scenario. If you have a list or a group of 500 people, then, you can expect around three to five of them to sign up.

As I've said before, it really is a numbers game. Of course, as I mentioned in the last chapter, you can have a way more engaged group and convert at a much higher rate, but these are the average figures. Do not launch too soon to a group of 100 and then be whacked over the head with the stick of disappointment when you are not raking in the cash.

If you have done everything in order, and have prepared properly, the launch is the most exciting time. It really should be enjoyable. So many people find it stress-inducing, but I love it. It's my favourite bit. The adrenaline is flowing, but I know have done everything I could possibly have done to make it a success.

Know, Like, Trust

There are loads of different ways to launch, but they all share a common goal: you are warming up your audience so they're ready to press the sign-me-up button. But to get them there, they have to like you. They have to feel you are the best-placed person to help them achieve what they need, and your product is the best way to get them to where they want to be – even if they don't currently have a very clear idea of where that may be. Because you will make sure they know their destination and then programme their satnav.

But you can't go in like a bull in a china shop. To use very old-fashioned language, you need to court them.

Take your time. Be patient.

There is a well-known phrase in the world of sales, which is: know/like/trust (KLT).

In the article 'Begin With Trust' by Harvard Business School professor Frances X. Frei and Anne Morriss, founder of the Leadership Consortium, it is stated that the three factors that build KLT are authenticity, logic and empathy:

- **Authenticity** is key because people must feel that they are hearing from the real you. If they don't believe this, there is very little chance that they will trust you. Remember, 'people buy from people', so keep that 'real-ness' at the forefront of all you do.

- **Logic** They are starting to like you because you are authentic and real, but they will still be asking themselves if they trust your logic, and if they can be reasonably sure (never 100 per cent sure – there are no magic fairies, remember) that you will get them a result, as they are potentially investing some of their hard-earned cash in you.
- **Empathy** Do you care about your potential clients? They need to see that you actually want them to succeed and that you are just playing a part in that success. The level of customer care you provide will be instrumental in this, as will your ethical approach. (There's a whole chapter on ethics coming up, but, suffice to say, your authenticity will have a huge impact on whether your empathy hits home with your ideal clients.)

Build Your Launch Plan

Put all relevant dates into your calendar, starting with the date you want your course/membership to begin and working backwards from that.

Then get everything done in advance. Remember, court them, woo them, spend time getting to know them, so they start to feel that they really know you. And like you.

1. THE WARM-UP

I usually recommend starting this phase about six weeks before the day you want people to buy your course or membership. (We call that day 'cart open')

Use videos, go live on social media, write posts – whatever best suits you, your personality and your audience – with the goal of educating your clients as to why they might need your service.

Remember, the trust element has to be further reinforced here, because you want them to trust your judgement and your knowledge. You do this by clearly outlining and describing the problem your ideal client has. This, in turn, will lead to the 'epiphany' moment when they think, Wow, that's exactly what is in my head; he/she really knows his/her stuff! The bond between you and them will start to be strengthened by this.

Examples

In Fabulous Foundations (FF, my business-basics course), I focus on not just 'spraying and praying' with marketing, where there's no strategy and instead you just spray marketing all over the place and pray it works. You try everything you can to get someone to buy your stuff – and sometimes they do, but you've done so much that you don't know what actually worked.

You see, I've been there, and because of that I can talk in my posts during the launch about how it feels, how frustrating it is and how it makes you want to quit having a business at all. Then my ideal client for the programme knows I totally get how they're feeling.

In my One To Many® programme launch, I talk about why working with one person at a time is so tricky. People are probably already flirting with the launch because they know they just don't have enough hours in the day to see all the clients who want to work with them one-to-one, so when I tell them there is another way to work that impacts more people in one go, they listen. They probably already know they need this. (Although sometimes they don't know and that's when education posts come in. I might say something like, 'How will you get paid if you are sick?' That reminds them that they have no back-up plan and that they need to start thinking about passive income.)

With the warm-up, you are basically educating people as to why they simply have to have your product.

2. THE EVENT

This is where you really want to up the engagement and get those prospective clients to think a bit deeper about what you are offering, how it would work for them and why *you* are the best person to help them. You are trying to further warm up your potential client by providing an event that they can take part in.

Again, there are loads of different ways to do this:

- Festival.
- Online summit.
- In-person summit.
- Bootcamp.
- Webinar.
- Sprint.
- Challenge.

All of the above work and people think of new ways to get people looking at them all the time, too.

Think about when Apple or Disney launch something. There is a buzz and they want all eyes on them for a period of time. This is the same.

Try to think of new ways that haven't been done yet to create a buzz.

I use a four-day challenge, where I create a pop-up Facebook group (one that is only there for the duration of the launch and then closes) and invite all potential clients to join. I present a thirty-minute lesson on each of the days. For instance, for my One To Many® programme, I have a challenge called 'Race To Recurring Revenue' and the lessons are about some of the things in this book – what your passive income stream could be, how to grow an audience, etc. At the end of each presentation, I set the members a challenge to complete, and they then post their results back into the group. This could be something like: tell us in five sentences who your ideal client is. This is great for getting your audience even more engaged and excited about what you can help them with, thus increasing engagement and also introducing an element of competition. (Because there are always prizes up for grabs.)

But more importantly, this starts to generate an atmosphere of peer support and collaboration. Participants will start sharing information and offering advice, thereby creating an environment that is representative of what will happen if they sign up.

A challenge is a great way to launch for a number of reasons:

- It gives people an opportunity to see if they like the way you teach, whether they think they could work with you and if you are compatible. It's another step on the KLT journey (see p. 166).

- By taking part in the challenge, they will have implemented some really useful content that will be a big part of moving forwards on their developmental journey. This means that they're already on the way to their goal, meaning they are clearer on the benefit of the next steps – i.e. to buy. If you hadn't opened their minds up by engaging them in the challenge, they may well have been too far removed from the content and value of your offer and therefore unlikely to make the investment. I see this a lot with passive income – people don't realise they can make money with the knowledge they already have, but by the end of the challenge they do.

- Those who take action will be more likely to join your course/membership, which is better for you as they are always more likely to do the work you set them – which means *they* get results and more people then buy the course.

- You will still be helping people to get results, even if they can't afford the programme. This is fantastic from a doing-the-right-thing perspective, but also means that the next time you launch, when they may be in a better position to buy up, they will remember you and your ethical/no-hard-sell approach and sign up.

TOP TIP

Don't forget you can get loads of great PR from the challenge stage:

- Make sure to create a hashtag so that people use it

on Instagram. This will get the attention of others who may join your group as a result.

- Show any great results on your sales page/Insta stories, so others can see that you get results.
- Show real responses, copied and pasted for authenticity (but block names out).
- Part of a challenge could be inviting five others to share the challenge with them – this very quickly gets more people involved.

3. THE MASTERCLASS

Next, I invite all those who have taken part in the event (and those who haven't) to a one-off masterclass, which will run for no longer than an hour.

This is an opportunity to delve deeper and give even more value to show that you are the expert. Make sure the masterclass covers the issues that your ideal client has. They need to see that you understand their problems and can solve them. An example could be 'Three reasons you are not getting clients' – this is a problem your ideal client has, and they will want to come to the masterclass to hear your solutions.

This is all leading up to the last ten minutes when you open the doors for enrolment.

How to set up your masterclass

About you There will be some people who just come in for this bit. You could say that they want the headline act not the support acts, so you will need to go over why you are the expert. Set out your credibility. Do not be afraid to brag. In England, we often see talking about ourselves and telling the truth about what we are good at as 'showing off'. Forget that. You need to be brimming with confidence and self-assurance. Your potential clients have to be sure that you are the one person who fully understands them and their problems and that you have the skills, experience and knowledge to help them to overcome them. They have to know you are the logical choice to purchase from because you are the expert in your industry. Someone once used the term 'Passive Income Queen' to describe me, and I liked it, so I use it. It doesn't say I'm '*an* expert'; rather, it says I am '*the* expert'. That is how you want to be seen.

- **The value piece** Now actually give them something for free that will be genuinely useful in achieving their goals. I suggest giving them five things they need to do. (When I do this, I show them my CASsH® system. This lays out the process of making passive income in five easy steps.) The first time I launched my FF business-basics course, I told them ten things – this is too many to give away, and no one signed up because they thought I had told them everything they needed to know. Marketers will often tell you to give potential clients the why and the what but not the how. I disagree. Tell them how. It won't stop them buying from you, as people come into programmes for more than just the knowledge.

- **The sell** You tell them how they can work with you further and open the doors to your course. You need confidence right now more than ever. Lots of people do the first steps really well, but get nervous and rush though this bit – because we all have an innate sense that selling is sleazy and we don't like doing it. Outline how they can do even more than they did in the challenge and the masterclass, and make sure you get interaction from your audience, so they are part of the process.

TOP TIP

At the beginning of the masterclass, give an incentive to stay until the end – a cheat sheet or a Q&A, for example, so they get to hear you sell.

- **The investment**: the last thing you'll talk about is the investment, but first you could give extra bonuses:
  - **Make sure you give the bonus a value** If you were to sell it on its own, what would the cost be?
  - **Only give bonuses that will help people get the results** the course or membership promises.
  - **Don't just throw in random free things** as this devalues what you are selling, rather than enhancing it.

You will then give them the link to a sales page to sign up if they want to. A sales page is a reminder of what the programme is all about and how much it costs and includes a button for them to pay. It stops you having to go back and forth on email with invoices.

4. LAUNCH WEEK

Once you've opened cart/started enrolment for your product, that is the official beginning of launch week.

You'll send an email to your list straight away (remember, you can automate this using a CRM system – see p. 150), making sure you are super visible, posting everywhere and getting yourself out there.

Make sure you email your list daily. It's better to do storytelling than sales emails here with links to buy. (Storytelling emails set the scene as to why the reader might need or want to buy the programme, rather than just giving factual sales information about the programme.) Clients will still want to see you as a real person, rather than a revenue-generating machine, so keep it personal. (Write these emails before you start launching, not as you go along. This is so helpful because it means you are available to be really on it, answering all the questions that could easily convert into sales if they are dealt with efficiently.)

Handle any worries about signing up with posts or lives on social media (wherever you are most comfortable) and ask for feedback on the main objections (concern that the programme will take too much time, for example).

You then close cart (stop people enrolling in the programme by closing the sales page off) five to seven days later, get a waitlist up for the next launch straight away and email your list saying it's too late to join this launch but they can get on the waitlist now.

Note: many people trot out the old classic 'We've added on an extra twenty-four to forty-eight hours before we close cart due to overwhelming demand'. *Do not do this*. It is a transparent attempt to improve a disappointing launch (I'm looking forward to discussing more of this sort of thing in the ethics chapter, coming up).

5. EVALUATE

I am well aware that this is the part no one wants to do because they're sick of all things 'launchy' by this point, but it's still so much a part of a successful launch.

First off, look at the metrics. Yep, I hate this word, too, because it makes me think of double maths at school, but you really do need to know this stuff for next time.

It's all about the percentages. Conversion rates, which I mentioned earlier, is the industry term. And it's quite simple, really. You get ten sign-ups from a list of 100 and you want fifty next time? Then you're going to need 500 on your list. Knowing your own personal conversion rate is brilliant because you can literally plan how much money you'll make next time.

Also, study every piece of information at your disposal:

- **Look at which emails worked/had the best conversion rates** Was one in particular an absolute killer – did you get a flurry of buyers after it went out? Look in your CRM system to see which emails got the most opens – this will usually be down to the subject line, so make a note of the good ones.
- **Consider what went right/wrong** For instance, did lots of people watch your masterclass to the end? Or

maybe not enough people opened the launch emails? Look back at all the stages and see what you can identify.

- **Do you need any help managing it all?** Were there periods when you couldn't cope with the level of questions coming in, for example? Or could you have used someone to help with writing the emails?
- **What did you learn?** Perhaps that you hate delivering challenges and would prefer to do a summit next time? Or that you need to write the emails much earlier?
- **Where were the gaps?** How many people went from each stage of the launch to the next? Where were the fallaways? How can you improve this?

The first time you launch a lot of work is required, and you may find yourself cursing me, thinking, Passive income? She's having a laugh! But the second, third and subsequent times, it most certainly is passive. You have created a viable product that you can sell over and over again, using the same marketing to the same audience.

I have launched on a Caribbean cruise and from a sun lounger in Las Vegas. It did not impact on my enjoyment. In fact, it actually made me relish the launches even more, knowing that what I was teaching was allowing me to take these amazing trips.

Affiliates

Once you've nailed launching, you can look at using friends and colleagues to sell your product to *their* audiences. They'll get a percentage of everything they sell, which can be as high as 50 per cent.

There are pros and cons to this system, and if you start to investigate it, you will find lots of people saying it definitely doesn't work. But I went from a £360k launch to a £2.5m launch using affiliates, so I am living proof that it can and does work. Nevertheless, it often gets a bad press, so here are a few pointers:

I wouldn't recommend diving straight in with an affiliate programme. Common sense dictates that you launch your course, membership or programme on your own at least three or four times, meaning that your audience and your reputation among your peers have grown sufficiently that those peers see selling your product as a profitable option for them.

If you do decide to use affiliates, make sure that your offering complements theirs – some people only ask affiliates who have worked with them, so they can say how good the course is. This might seem obvious, but you really need your values to chime with those of the people who are being sold to in other groups.

Following on from this, think carefully about whether to use lots of affiliates with small audiences or fewer with larger audiences, bearing in mind that a big audience doesn't automatically mean an engaged one.

Help your affiliates by training in their groups, so their audience gets to know you. Be clear about why you are working with them and talk about the values and goals that you share. This will make the job of selling your product in their group much easier for them.

If you have done well enough in your own launches to make an affiliate programme viable, there is some really useful software out there to help you keep track of payments, etc. This is definitely worth investing in.

Exercise: Getting ready to launch

- If you already have an audience either on social media or an email list, work out your conversion rate based on 2 per cent (yours might end up being higher). How many people would buy a course that you launched right now?
- Sign up for some launches. Search social media for summits, challenges or masterclasses. Study them to see how they're done. What do you like about them? What don't you like?
- If you sign up for the launch events, you'll then receive the daily launch emails. Store them. You can read them for inspiration when it comes to your own launch. I have a folder of hundreds of people's launch emails and another folder for emails I particularly connected with.
- Start writing your own launch emails, or at least bullet pointing what your readers will need to know about your programme – and why. Are there some stories you could add to make your point clearer?

CHAPTER 9
The Only Way is Ethics

In my first year in my strategy business, I decided to hire some coaches. I'd heard they can really help to up your game and I wanted to do the very best I could. I ended up working with three.

One of them was someone I thought would be great. He was what you'd call an old-timer (maybe a boomer, if you're young enough to call people boomers) who had been running an online business for a fairly long time. He was also feisty and to the point and I generally like that. But he was *really* expensive (I'm talking tens of thousands of pounds), which I'd have to take out of the profit of my very-new-but-doing-ok business.

I decided to introduce him to Sam (my husband is much better at listening to intuition than I am). He immediately told me not to work with this person. He described him as a 'Del-boy snake-oil salesperson' and said he was not to be trusted.

I decided, as I generally do, to ignore Sam. This man was making millions, so of course he was going to be a bit salesy and come across a bit weird. I'd love to tell you that I was right, but unfortunately I was not.

After spending a bit of time with him, having handed over my money, it was clear there had been some exaggeration in the finances department. I also saw some pretty dodgy things happening behind the scenes in his business, which left me feeling very uneasy. And as for him teaching me anything, I learned nothing.

The first time I went to meet him, he was nearly an hour late, as he was discussing something in the garden with his housekeeper. The second time, he asked me to do a pitch in front of him while he took notes to help me. I quite liked this idea – at least it was an actionable task. But while I pitched away and he (supposedly) made notes, he forgot there was a large mirror behind him in which I could see him answering emails and chatting to friends. I could have pitched a flying pig and he wouldn't have noticed. He also brought a camera to a session we had on a retreat and asked me to give a testimonial there and then in front of people. I felt intimidated and obliged to do it.

I ended up skipping our last sessions and chalking it up to experience, through which I learned how *not* to run my business. We live and learn.

A couple of months later, someone I barely knew asked me if she should hand over a great deal of money to work with this person. She had seen my testimonial but felt something was 'off' and wanted to hear from me personally.

I felt very conflicted. Should I say the coach was a complete waste of money and risk him coming after me? Or should I lie and say it was a worthwhile investment, knowing this could negatively impact others? In the end, I settled for somewhere in the middle, but a week later all hell broke loose. The coach had got wind of my testimonial and rallied his clients and industry friends, some of whom I knew and liked.

Three threads then appeared in three different Facebook groups and pages slating a new coach who was teaching business and who used to be a wedding planner. The posts didn't name me, but they didn't have to. It was classic school-bullying behaviour. And I should know!

I'd like to tell you that I fought back immediately. But I did not. I hid. I decided I did not want to be in an industry where things like this happened. Then, after a few days of it all getting steadily worse, I contacted a lawyer. He told me that I had to 'out' myself because the coach and his minions were clearly enjoying being in the powerful position of being able to name me whenever they felt like it.

I was terrified but I did a Facebook live telling everyone that the threads they had all read were about me, that none of it was true and that we were going down the legal route.

Suddenly, I got hundreds of messages from people apologising, saying they would never have commented if they'd have known it was about me (why don't people not comment anyway when they only hear one side?) and many others telling me the coach had behaved badly to them, too, but they hadn't dared to speak out.

The coach was told by my lawyers to take the posts down and never to talk about me again.

But what of the coach himself? After pursuing things legally that first year, he told me he would make sure that I never worked in the industry again, that he had friends in high places within the industry and that nobody else would work with me either.

That's all it took for me to go on to make multiple millions of pounds, overtaking him financially much quicker than I would have done otherwise.

There's always a silver lining eh!

The Emperor's New Clothes

When you create a business that can only thrive with you being visible (remember that word? You'd better!) on the Internet, the chances are you will enter it with a lovely naivety, thinking about the wonderful things you will achieve and the amazing, supportive and inspirational people you will meet.

But the blinkers soon come off and you start to get a whiff of something.

My eye opening came about as a result of the story you've just read, and, while it did shatter my innocence, it also put me on a much firmer footing for negotiating the pitfalls that running an online business inevitably dumps in your path. (My love/hate relationship with this industry continues to this day.)

Earlier on I talked about the dark side, and this is inherently related to that. We'll call it 'the manipulative side'. It's a bit taboo. You don't hear it talked about much, because . . . well . . . strong, sometimes unpopular opinions can lose you clients.

Ok, here we go.

COMPETITION AND COMPARING

Many business owners fear competition. But I hope that by this stage of the book, you have read and learned enough to have absorbed the very basic and sensible approach that supporting others does not impact your success.

Success is not pizza – there is plenty to go around!

And while you might hear 'community over competition' reeled off daily online by all and sundry, it very often tends to mean 'community over competition – until I have some competition, at which point community can do one'.

If you say it, mean it. Live it. The sentiment and the message are spot on, but actions speak louder than soundbites.

Try to keep this little reminder at the forefront of your mind:

- Don't snipe – applaud.
- Don't envy – compliment.
- Don't compare – respect.
- Don't imitate – innovate.

BRO MARKETING

We touched on this earlier (see p. 17), but it's worth mentioning again here.

Bro marketing (a term that doesn't just refer to techniques used by men) describes the old-school sales methods we all find a bit unsavoury. (I say 'all' in the hope that because you've stuck with me this long, you'll be sharing my thoughts here). It uses tactics that get to the bits of you that are vulnerable, so you will be far more readily manipulated, and therefore easier to sell to. (**Note:** this is not a new way of selling.)

It targets natural human triggers and reactions. For example, make something scarce or say that it's going to stop being available soon, and we all start to get a bit twitchy. 'What if everyone else gets it and I miss out?' We make decisions based on the wrong reasons.

Bro marketing works especially well with low-ticket offers because we're much more likely to say, 'Oh sod it, why not?' and less likely to ask the important questions about whether the product is really what we need.

Another example is when influencers and entrepreneurs show you pics of themselves with their gold-plated Bentleys or outside their multi-million-dollar seafront homes. Do not trust these posts. Often, they are carefully stage-managed with props and hired cars to project a certain image.

MANIPULATIVE MARKETING TECHNIQUES

We hear of FOMO (fear of missing out) in so many contexts, but did you know it's one of the biggest ways to sell to people? FOMO and trauma marketing feed into your insecurities, using your existing traumas, such as being left out or feeling you don't fit in. If you feel you never belong because you had a bad time at school, for example, then when a coach tells you everyone else is joining their new membership and you're going to be missing out, your subconscious is going to want to buy in, regardless of whether or not you can afford it or need it.

INVISIBLE OFFERS AND GIMMICKS

When I was ten, my dad took me to a market. A man with a cockney accent was on one of the stalls, telling people he was going to put thousands of pounds' worth of things into a box and sell it to one person for £30. Everyone was dubious, but someone bought it. We all crowded round to see what was in the box. There was a watch worth loads and some other expensive things. It was a bargain.

The guy then said he was going to make some more 'ghost offers' of items in boxes. He stressed the boxes would all contain different things but be worth more than £30. All the hands shot up, including my dad's (and he did not have £30 to spare).

When the boxes were opened there was disappointment all round. Gone were the expensive watches and luxury items. All we had was some old perfume and a dodgy ornament. But we'd been warned that anything could be in the box, so we couldn't get a refund. It was simply a scam. A gimmick. And once it became known that the first guy who got the amazing box was actually a plant and the main geezer's mate, the whole ghost-offers enterprise became illegal.

Until someone decided to bring it into the online world and rename it invisible offers. Nowadays, it goes like this: a coach sells a course but does not tell you what it is about or if you need it – only that it is worth more than they are selling it for. The FOMO part of you wants that course. What if everyone else gets it and you don't?

But wait – they add another layer of manipulation. Let's say the price goes up every day. Now you really want in because you will get it for £111 whereas someone else might pay £777 further down the line. Again, this will be justified as the coach wanting the course to be affordable to everyone (even though if that was true, they'd keep it at the low price).

One of the biggest issues for entrepreneurs is managing their spend and buying the products they need to grow their business. But with ghost offers, they have no idea if they need what's on offer because they don't know what it is. The only reason to buy it, then, is fear – which is exactly what trauma marketing is about.

SHAME MARKETING

This has become extremely popular online, especially when selling to women. If you tell an online seller you're not buying something because you can't afford it, you'll be told in no uncertain terms to put it on a credit card – otherwise it shows you clearly don't believe in yourself or your business. This is emotional manipulation dressed up as empowerment.

And don't even think of saying you need to talk it over with a partner – then you'll really be shamed. You see, you're not a real business if you have to make decisions with someone else.

THE CONSTANT UPSELL METHOD

Here's how this one goes:

You buy a course. You get a couple of weeks to take it (no lifetime access here). You realise very quickly there's no way you'll have time to watch the course in two weeks. Then the marketer says you can have an extra two weeks if you shout about how amazing the course is all over your social media (yeah, the course you haven't even looked at yet). And you do it because you don't want to waste your money.

As you near the end of the course, you are then sold the next month's course – because this one will only really help you in conjunction with the next one. And you buy it.

Then, the exact same thing happens again, and after month three, you're told you might as well buy the entire year's courses at a cost of thousands of pounds, as it will end up saving you money.

So many of my clients have bought a year's worth of courses, and never got to watch a single thing because of the two-weeks-only rule. But they kept buying in the hope that they'd at least get *something* for the money they've paid.

USING NLP AND HYPNOSIS TO SELL

Neuro-linguistic programming has become popular since it started in the 1970s, and is a way of changing someone's thoughts and behaviours to help achieve desired outcomes for them. It operates through the conscious use of language to influence someone's thoughts and decision making.

NLP (and hypnosis) can be used for good. I've used both to help change how I think about the bullying in my childhood, for example, and there are some brilliant practitioners out there. But it can be used online as a manipulative way to sell, and nobody seems to talk about this.

Quite a few people have told me they've bought programmes they don't need and that aren't even very good. Some told me they've provided testimonials and posted on threads, saying how great the programmes are, but that they don't understand why they felt so compelled to support them in this way. When questioned as to why they purchased the programmes they told me they bought them, uncharacteristically, without doing any research and feel 'stupid' having done so. Mostly, they bought impulsively, without even looking at a sales page. In fact, most times there *was* no sales page.

I did some research and found that there are entire books and studies on how to use NLP and hypnosis to make suggestions to a person's subconscious. In the context of online sales, I think it comes down to your interpretation of what is happening here: is it influence or is it manipulation?

NLP Academy, 'the global leader for NLP excellence', states: 'A sales-person trained in NLP knows how to communicate in such a way that engages the thinking processes of a client to stimulate the decision, the action, the behaviour and the state required for that person to become a client and feel good about the choice.'*

This will always be a subjective view, and I leave it to you to form your own, but it's certainly something worth

---

* Taken from NLP Academy website: https://www.nlpacademy.co.uk/articles/view/what_is_neuro_linguistic_selling/

thinking about and being aware of when operating in the online world (and beyond).

LYING AND EXAGGERATING ON SOCIALS

You will hear loads of people online calling themselves six- or seven-figure entrepreneurs.

Firstly, you should check what currency their sales are being measured in (FYI, 100,000 Japanese yen equals around £612). Also, check exactly what they actually mean by 'seven-figure business owner'. My understanding of this term is that the seven-figure milestone has been achieved within the space of a year. But some people will use it to mean they have turned over seven figures since starting their business, be that twelve months or twelve years ago.

Use your due diligence and ask the questions. Never be afraid to ask for proof of anything the marketer is saying if you're about to hand over money.

The issue with all the tactics I've described is that once one well-known coach uses them, they're seen as ok by every-one in their audience, so then they all follow suit, so creating a dishonest and unethical industry.

Transparency

Talking about money and how much you earn is ok. Yes, even in the UK, where money seems to be a dirty word. In fact, it's important to show people what's possible and take away the taboo around the subject – but why not go further and show exactly how you have earned it, so people can learn from you?

It is so important to be transparent here. I regularly share my online bank statement, as this shows my ins and outs. I also talk about the percentages that come from each of my products, and any investment I need to make in them – in terms of both time and money. And I tell everyone I work with to ask me as many questions as they can think of – as do I, if I am going to invest in someone's services.

Copying and Plagiarism

If you're good at what you do online, prepare to be copied.

I've had entire courses, challenges and posts copied. Most people will change a word or a sentence here or there before copying everything else, but one woman last year neglected to change anything when she lifted my posts and so gave herself a husband named Sam in her posts! I've also seen slogans I've made up printed on T-shirts with no credit to me. And I've even had my entire backstory copied by someone who grew up with millions, but thought my humble origins were selling my products.

> ## Be inspired by what you see/read, but never copy. Words are livelihoods in the online space.

People tell me I should be flattered. But I'm not flattered when others steal my work. And neither should you be.

If you are copied, remember two things:

1 Nobody else can ever be you.

2 Copyright law exists for a reason. Use it! There are some great online lawyers out there who will help you protect your stuff.

Defamation

Let's face it. People will sometimes lie about business owners online. This is called defamation. And business owners are often afraid of being visible online in case this happens to them, but don't let it scare you. The law is on your side when it comes to defamation and there are things you can do.

There are lawyers who are specialists in dealing with this area, but it all starts with a cease and desist. This is a document you can send to the person who is lying to say that if they don't take down their lies, you will take it further and seek legal support. This is usually enough to make them see sense, but if not, getting a lawyer is your next step. If you do go down this road, you could be awarded damages if the lies have harmed your business (I've been through it and it's not as scary as it sounds).

A Word on Integrity

I believe the biggest threat to the online industry is the reputation it's giving itself.

People are resorting more and more to desperate, unethical ways to get people to buy things. And the saddest thing is, they don't need to. Because, quite simply, if you have knowledge that someone else needs, they will buy it, as my case study below proves.

In my first year of business, when I became aware of all the dodgy things happening online, I told my mentor I didn't think I could be in an industry that fosters such unethical practices. And you know what she told me? She said, 'You can leave or you can change the industry from the inside. Make so much money while retaining your integrity that people sit up and notice that it can be done.'

And so that's what I've been doing. And I hope this book has a ripple effect, so that all you readers show others it can be done, too.

VISIBLE LAUNCH CASE STUDY – *MY STORY*

I am the case study this time!

Recently, my team and I did an experiment. We discussed whether it would be possible to have a six-figure launch using no 'salesy' techniques and just telling people about a brand-new programme.

We called it Visible. And it does what it says on the tin. We hoped to be able to show that you *can* make money this way.

And we did it. With no ads, a brand-new offering, one of my lowest-priced products ever and not even the slightest dodgy marketing tactics. And I had a multi-six-figure launch. (In £UK, if you need to know!)

I'm prouder of this launch than any multi-seven-figure launch I've ever had because it confirmed something I already knew: that you can sell in a way that makes you feel good and still have great financial success.

We can do it differently.
Ethically. With integrity.

Exercise: Knowing your values

Get a pen and paper and devise your own 'Ethics Plan' for your existing business or the one you are planning. Ask yourself questions like these:

- What are my fundamental values?
- How do I want my client or customer to feel?
- How do I want to sell?
- What sales methods do I definitely not want to use?
- Then think about businesses or entrepreneurs that you like and respect and look at how they approach selling.
- Do they align with you?
- What can you learn from them?
- What do you think would be an improvement on their values?

Final Words

It is said (and I'm not sure by whom) that there are a million ways to make a million dollars. I think that's true. And making money online is a great choice.

We are so lucky to be here on this earth at a time when technology has made it possible to do everything with just a laptop. Just a few years ago it would have blown my mind if someone had told me that I would make lots of money helping people to live a life they absolutely love – and that I could do it while travelling the world with my family. But that is now my reality, and there's absolutely no reason why it cannot be yours, too.

This book has been a whistle-stop tour of the best types of passive and semi-passive income streams but I hope it's shown you a couple of things:

1. Making money online is not just for a certain 'type' of person. Because it doesn't matter if you're Bartholomew from Belgravia or Betty from Barnsley – everyone has knowledge they can sell and can make money in this way if they know what to do.

2. When it comes to any kind of business – on- or off-line – two things matter: having a strategy (yours is in this book) and making sure you have the right mindset to take action.

Starting anything new like this takes time and patience, though, and can be really overwhelming. So try to take it step by step. Don't rush it – it's not a race – and you'll soon look back and see how all the steps you've put into place are creating an amazing business.

I'm so excited for you to be on this journey. Keep me updated with how you're getting on and remember that if someone like me has changed their life so dramatically in just five years, you definitely can, too!

Resources

Books and Audiobooks

Atomic Habits: An Easy and Proven Way to Build Good Habits and Break Bad Ones – James Clear (Penguin Audio)

Get Rich, Lucky Bitch! Release Your Money Blocks and Live a First-Class Life – Denise Duffield-Thomas (CreateSpace Independent Publishing Platform)

She Means Business – Carrie Green (Hay House UK)

Superfans: The Easy Way to Stand Out, Grow Your Tribe, and Build a Successful Business – Pat Flynn (Flynndustries LLC)

The E-Myth Revisited: Why Most Small Businesses Don't Work and What to Do About It – Michael E. Gerber (Harper Audio)

Profit First: Transform Your Business from a Cash-Eating Monster to a Money-Making Machine – Mike Michalowicz (Gildan Media LLC)

*You Are a Badass At Making Money: Master the Mindset of
    Wealth* – Jen Sincero (audiobook, John Murray)
Start With Why – Simon Sinek (Penguin Audio)

Podcasts

The Lucky Bitch by Denise Duffield-Thomas – for all things
    money mindset
The Spencer Lodge Podcast – for all things investing and
    money
The Email Marketing Show by Rob and Kennedy – for all
    things funnels
On Purpose With Alex Beadon – for all things online
    business
Smart Passive Income Podcast with Pat Flynn – for passive
    income tips

Acknowledgments

Writing the acknowledgments has been the hardest part of writing this book because too many people have helped along the way. You don't build a multi-million-pound business alone – there are so many people who have inspired and helped me.

To Geeta Nanda – for starting me off and allowing me to see that women could be successful *and* kind. You saw a potential that I'm not sure I saw in myself.

To the various people that have inspired me and given me great advice at different times – from five years ago, when I first opened that Facebook group, to now, including, but nowhere near limited to Denise Duffield-Thomas, Selena Soo, Emily and James Williams, Natalie MacNeil, Niyc Pidgeon, Carrie Green, Ron Reich, Spencer Lodge and Bushra Azhar. I am so aware that in everything I have been able to achieve, I'm standing on the shoulders of giants who have already lit up the pathway.

To those who help my mindset whenever trying to force this industry to develop more integrity becomes a lot to carry – Charlotte Carter, Caroline Strawson, Kim Raine and Shari Teigman; you've all saved my sanity more than once and made me think about why others do the things they do.

To my little team, who despite being friends and family are brilliant at challenging me. It's always needed and your input into everything, including this book, is always appreciated. And Zoe – thanks for making things happen when health decides I can't.

To my very first reader – Nova Cobban: thanks for volunteering to stay up and read it all in one sitting. Your perspective really helped.

To Linda and everyone at BulliesOut – thanks for giving me a place where I can do some good. What you all do is amazing!

To Holly Whitaker and everyone at Yellow Kite – you've made this process so enjoyable. I'd heard horror stories of demanding editors, but you've been a joy.

To my friends who have made the term 'business friends' unnecessary, because while I may have met you because of the business, we are now so much more than that – Dani, Deep, Monique, Charlie, Shelly, Jonelle, Amanda, Lauren, Abi, Nicola, Inge and so many others. I'm lucky I get to share work and play with you.

To my clients – you're why I do this and your messages about how your lives have changed are what make me continue when it gets tough. I attract the best clients in the world.

To my 'before-any-of-this-happened' friends – I continue to appreciate you more than you know. Thanks for grounding me and not allowing me to become a complete idiot. You are the reason I've not changed and never will. Karen and Andy, Jen and Kris, Lois and Kieran and Joy.

To my two besties:

Hazel – thanks for being not only a fabulous best friend but also my memory for everything in childhood. I still don't know how you recall every tiny little thing. V and L wouldn't stand a chance if they saw us now! Thanks for giving up your job to come work for me.

Paulie – you got there first with the book writing but I got more credit! Thanks for being a constant presence when I needed one throughout so much stuff over the past twenty years.

To Darren Bell – who really wanted to write the Foreword. I promised you'd be in the book and there you are! I hope you're not too disappointed.

Thanks have to go to my sister who is there by my side through all of it, who tells me when I'm in the wrong but sticks up for me anyway and who has had my back since she pushed sixteen-year-old hard-boy Jeremy into a wall aged thirteen when he was bullying me. I love that we now get to work together and go on this crazy ride together. Who knew this was where we'd end up when we talked in that little council-house bedroom on Essex Road about what our lives would look like?

To my family in Lincolnshire, Malta and everywhere else you're scattered – thanks for being supportive in all this and cheering me on. It means a lot to know I can rely on you all.

To Mum – thanks for giving me the confidence to be a strong woman who dares use her voice and who always stands up for those who cannot. People may have said you were argumentative, too much, too loud, intimidating. I saw a person who knew what they wanted and would fight for the underdog, who stood up for what they believed in and who got back up, time and time again, no matter how hard it was. It's rubbed off.

To Dad – for telling me I can be anything and do anything, for listening to no excuses, for instilling in me a work ethic like no other and for writing me a letter when I turned eighteen that stayed with me and eventually changed my direction for good.

To my little boys, Finnian and Albert, who aren't so little any more. You two are my real inspiration. All of it is really for you. Keep making me as proud as you do now.

But mostly to Sam. None of this would have happened without you. None of it. It's no coincidence that my life started to drastically change for the better the minute you walked into it. I love you more – and now it's official because it's in a book! Being a team of two makes none of it as scary as it could be. Let's see what new adventures await in the next five years.

About the Author

credit Amanda Karen Photography

Lisa Johnson is a multi-seven-figure global business strategist who makes 90 per cent of her money through passive or semi-passive income streams. In one launch alone during the global pandemic in 2021 she made £2.5m in a week, earning £1m in the first hour of sales, with continued success in 2022 when she made £2.2m in another week. Her consulting business made over £10m in the first five years.

After a tough childhood, living in social housing, Lisa went on to have successful careers in law and banking. Her experience in overcoming obstacles has helped to mould her into a bold, straight-talking coach, who is never afraid to be an authentic and outspoken truth teller. In just five years, Lisa took herself from £30,000 in debt to making millions as a successful entrepreneur, helping thousands of people.

Lisa has over 50,000 followers across social media and a number-1 business podcast, *Making Money Online*, which has listeners in 119 countries and over 150,000 downloads to date. She has appeared on the BBC's *Woman's Hour* and has been featured in national newspapers and magazines, including the *Telegraph*, *Psychologies*, the *Guardian* and *Fast Company*. A piece on Lisa in *Forbes* magazine garnered over a quarter of a million views in one week.

Lisa is a huge believer that everyone can become a success, no matter their background. She is an ambassador for the charity BulliesOut and is known for her anti-bullying campaigning online.

Lisa lives in Bedfordshire, UK with her husband and twin sons, but consults across the globe.

Index

yellow kite

books to help you live a good life

Join the conversation and tell
us how you live a #goodlife

🐦 @yellowkitebooks
📘 YellowKiteBooks
📌 Yellow Kite Books
📷 YellowKiteBooks